MW00345583

The Fast Track
Formula

Books that make you better

Books that make you better. That make you *be* better, *do* better, *feel* better. Whether you want to upgrade your personal skills or change your job, whether you want to improve your managerial style, become a more powerful communicator, or be stimulated and inspired as you work.

Prentice Hall Business is leading the field with a new breed of skills, careers and development books. Books that are a cut above the mainstream – in topic, content and delivery – with an edge and verve that will make you better, with less effort.

Books that are as sharp and smart as you are.

Prentice Hall Business.
We work harder – so you don't have to.

For more details on products, and to contact us, visit
www.pearsoned.co.uk

ALAN ROBERTSON

The Fast Track
Formula

How to accelerate your career

PEARSON
Prentice Hall
BUSINESS

London • New York • Toronto • Sydney • Tokyo • Singapore • Hong Kong
Cape Town • New Delhi • Madrid • Paris • Amsterdam • Munich • Milan

PEARSON EDUCATION LIMITED

Edinburgh Gate
Harlow CM20 2JE
Tel: +44 (0)1279 623623
Fax: +44 (0)1279 431059
Website: www.pearsoned.co.uk

First published in Great Britain in 2004

© Pearson Education Limited 2004

The right of Alan Robertson to be identified as author of this work has been asserted by him in accordance with the Copyright, Designs and Patents Act 1988.

ISBN 0 273 67550 8

British Library Cataloguing-in-Publication Data
A catalogue record for this book is available from the British Library

Library of Congress Cataloging-in-Publication Data

Robertson, Alan.
    The fast track formula : how to accelerate your career / Alan Robertson.
        p. cm.
    ISBN 0-273-67550-8 (alk. paper)
        1. Career development. 2. Success in business. I. title.

    HF5381.R66 2004
    650.1--dc22

                                                                2004040071

All rights reserved. No part of this publication may be reproduced, stored in a retrieval system, or transmitted in any form or by any means, electronic, mechanical, photocopying, recording or otherwise, without either the prior written permission of the publisher or a licence permitting restricted copying in the United Kingdom issued by the Copyright Licensing Agency Ltd, 90 Tottenham Court Road, London W1T 4LP. This book may not be lent, resold, hired out or otherwise disposed of by way of trade in any form of binding or cover other than that in which it is published, without the prior consent of the Publishers.

10 9 8 7 6 5 4 3 2 1
08 07 06 05 04

Typeset in 10.5 pt Minion by 70
Printed and bound in Great Britain by Bell & Bain Ltd, Glasgow

The publisher's policy is to use paper manufactured from sustainable forests.

**For Mark and Katie, Richard and Sarah,
at the threshold of your careers**

Thanks to ...

Many friends and acquaintances, long-standing and more recent, have contributed to making this book better than it would otherwise have been. My thanks to all of them for contributing the insights, observations and other benefits of their experience. They should shoulder none of the blame for what I have made of their inputs, but certainly share any credit.

Graham Abbey, Sally Atkinson, Richard Clayton, Jonathan Crookall, Charlie Dalgleish, David Dorman, Paul Gaskin, Marilyn Hoffman, Claire Holloway, Stephen Huntley, Mike Konig, Dana Lawrence, Susanne Parsons, Sandi Paterson, Paul Pelosi and Connie Ristic

Special thanks to ...

Kevin Eyre for the original conversation – and many of the subsequent ones – that eventually led to this book

David Perkins and Shari Tishman at Harvard Project Zero for introducing me to much of what I have learned about higher-order thinking

Lindsay Mair, a long way from the Gascon wine trade, but still working in the same spirit

Rachael Stock for her advice, guidance and expertise as a publisher

And above all love and thanks to

Hilary for once again providing patient, challenging and creative support throughout the whole endeavour

Acknowledgements ...

Extracts from *Villenueve: Winning in Style* are reprinted by permission of HarperCollins Publishers Ltd. © Jacques Villeneuve with Gerald Donaldson (1997)

Extracts from *Losing My Virginity: the autobiography* by Richard Branson are reprinted by permission of Virgin Books Ltd. © Richard Branson (1998)

Extracts from *Open Secret* by Stella Rimington published by Hutchinson. Used by permission of The Random House Group Limited

Extracts from *Momentum: the struggle for peace, politics & the people* reproduced by permission of Hodder and Stoughton Limited (2002)

Contents

Introducing ...
An ambitious little book

Like you, this little book has ambitions. More precisely, it has four.

First, to prise open the phrase 'career progression' and take a close look at what this involves in practice. The aim is to uncover what really propels careers, and to reveal which factors are the most significant accelerators. What is the 'Fast Track Formula'?

Secondly, and most importantly, to provide advice that is simultaneously well-grounded and highly practical. Strong pointers, based on sound understandings, that will enable you to propel your career faster. To show how the fast-track formula can be applied.

Thirdly, to give you an opportunity to think more deeply about what comes with career progression, and about what you might ultimately want from your own. A chance to reflect on the broader implications, not just the rewards, of career advancement. How fast and how far do you want to go?

Finally, to be concise. To be an ambitious *little* book. Time is precious. The demands on our time, and attention, are many. So this book aims to be sufficient rather than to saturate, and to be provocative rather than definitive, some carefully chosen words on the subject rather than the last word.

A provocative proposition

Claiming to offer a 'fast track formula' is deliberately provocative. Is there a 'formula' that permits career acceleration? Yes. Is it a complex formula? Surprisingly not. Why then is it not general knowledge? Careers are hardly new. No, but they are not generally well understood, except in retrospect, and sometimes not even then. And, if you want to accelerate your career, you need the formula in advance, in mind as you go forward. The problem is that the formula is not so much complex as un-obvious. Until it is drawn to your attention.

So, in the spirit of getting quickly to the point, here is a preview of the Fast Track Formula, the ingredients for accelerating a career.

A rapid grasp of context
plus
a capacity for higher-order thinking
plus
higher-order interpersonal skills
produce
faster and continuing career progression

This is the proposition. It is not to say that nothing else affects the advancement of a career. Other factors can and do. But they do not influence career progression so greatly. This book concentrates on the factors that make the biggest contribution. The ones that are essentially within your control. The ones which most deserve your attention.

However, the answer without the explanation is going to be of limited usefulness, so here are some pointers about what follows.

The shape of things to come

To make a formula work, you have to understand all the ingredients, and also how to put them together. So that is how this book is organized, in four parts.

Part One, The Nature of the Track, is about having a grasp of context, about understanding the course. Neither jobs nor careers take place in a vacuum. In any arena in which you are called upon to perform, context will have an important bearing on outcomes. The absence of that understanding commonly causes careers to falter and fail. Fast-tracking requires a sharp appreciation of context and its implications for performance.

Part Two, Mental Agility, is about higher-order thinking, about power and steering. Like most competitive tracks, careers don't simply proceed in straight lines. They are full of twists, turns and gradients that need to be negotiated. It's not a case of hitting top speed, setting cruise control and relaxing. Different roles, different moments and different parts of the track need you to be in different gears and actively steering. You need to have the gears, and know when and how to use them, to get the most out of your power.

Part Three, Interaction, is about higher-order interpersonal skills, about taking others with you. Like other competitive tracks, careers always involve spectators and judges, fans and critics, not to mention other drivers. You can't declare yourself a fast-tracker. That accolade always depends on the opinions – and behaviour – of other people. So this part of the formula, and the book, is concerned with how you relate, the impression that you make on others, whether other people on the track allow you to proceed. Above all, this is to do with how you conduct yourself in relation to others at certain defining moments. Knowing when as well as knowing how.

Part Four, The Formula at Work, is about pulling the ingredients together, about using all this know-how in reality. In that respect careers are unlike any other competitive track. The career course is extraordinarily long. Even other long-distance tests of endurance like the Le Mans 24-hour, or the Monte Carlo Rally, are sprints by comparison. Seeing the route is harder when the course is so largely unmarked, more like an off-road event than a grand prix. Recognizing a wrong turn is harder. Recognizing the implications, and correcting for the consequences of a wrong turn, are harder still. The longer the course, the trickier it is to stay alert. This part of the book is about staying alert over a long-haul.

Assumptions

I have made a few assumptions.

I assume that what brings you to this book is that you want your career to progress and desire that progress to be faster than average, not slower.

I assume that your work is primarily mental rather than physical. That it is, as a growing majority of jobs are in the developed economies of the twenty-first century, essentially concerned with knowledge work, with the acquisition, manipulation and utilization of information. Beyond that, I make no assumption either about what sort of career you are in, or whereabouts you are in it. This book has been written to be of relevance and use, whatever your career domain, whether you are in the early stages or in the middle of it, whether you are eager or bewildered, anxious or enthusiastic about your prospects.

Wherever your career, and wherever you are in it, I assume that you want something that will give you an edge. So this book concentrates on finding and revealing edges: the significant edge of others' experience; the edge of relevant research and thinking; the edge of your own capabilities; the edge that comes from attending to the small things that make the big differences.

Let's get to it.

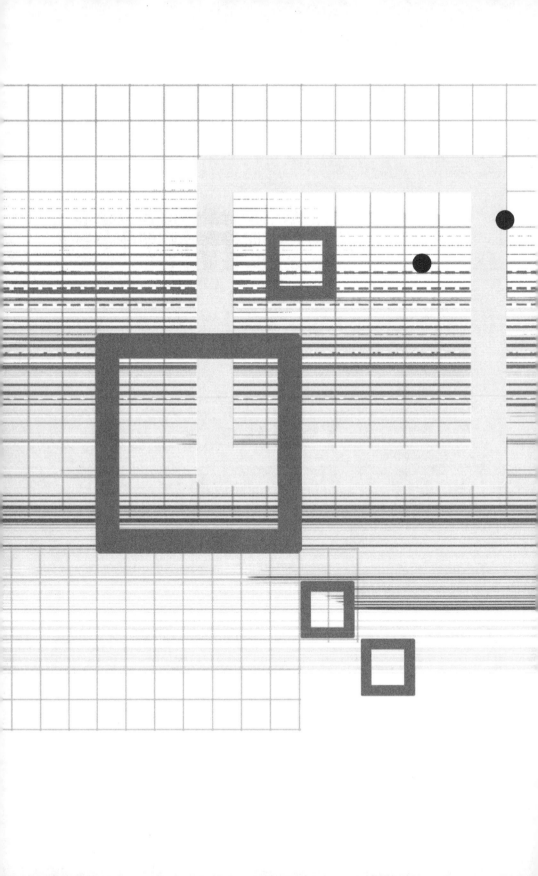

1

PART ONE
The Nature of the Track

CHAPTER ONE

Careering Along

'Career progression.' The phrase sounds smooth. The reality isn't.

The purpose of this chapter is to provide an antidote to the attraction of search consultants' overtures, the allure of recruiters' advertising copy and the glossy enticements of graduate recruitment brochures. Steering a career is not the straightforward process that phrases like 'excellent career prospects' and 'outstanding development opportunities' would have you believe. On the contrary, the process needs to be negotiated in every sense of the word. It is only partially within your control.

But we are living in what has been dubbed the era of 'career self-reliance', dominated by the notion that individuals are now responsible for their own continuing 'employability'. In that case, even before you start putting your foot on what you hope is the accelerator, you'd better have some under-standing about the nature of careers and how to handle them. Which also means knowing something about the track.

A career is a strange journey.

- You set off without really knowing where you'll end up.
- You want to proceed, but don't know what that will require you to do.
- Much of the time you can't see the road or where you're heading.
- You want to go fast, but sometimes you don't even seem to be moving.
- It quickly becomes apparent that careers aren't easy to steer.
- Much of the time you don't feel in control.

- What you thought was the accelerator can turn out to be the brake.

- The journey can be bumpy, uncomfortable and liable to accident.

- You may not be sure when, or even whether, you've arrived.

How many other journeys would you embark on under such conditions? But this is the nature of the track. Understanding the track is therefore a significant part of the challenge that you face in accelerating your career.

A glance in the mirror

On any journey it's a smart move to glance in the mirror from time to time. To see what's going on around you. So here's a selection of people describing the experience of their careers. One reason for including these comments is to illustrate what careers are really like, as people live them. Careering along. The other reason is to encourage you to reflect on your own career, so that you can more quickly relate and apply what you find in this book to your own particular circumstances and needs. You'll find some questions to prompt your reflections after each extract.

Let's hear first from a Marketing Director, now retired, but successful enough to do so by the time he was fifty. How does he describe his career?

If it was a graph, showing my stock price, it would be podium step shape with a slow start, a plateau, and a slow end. At the time it seemed like a series of challenges, mostly getting bigger and mostly slightly different in nature. We (my peers and I) used to talk about it a lot in terms of hierarchy (how far we had got up the organogram, how far we would get). Later I saw it as a series of boxes to have ticked off. For example, marketing functions to have worked in (advertising, research, sales, product development, etc.). Or geographical areas to have worked in (UK, Far East, Latin America, Europe, Africa). Or even vices (I've done booze and fags, so next it would need to be white-slaving or class A drugs. Joking, by the way!). Within that there was a sort of calendar or cycle. Each step had its own series of challenges or entertainment, and you might do these two or three times before you got good at it, or boredom set in, and one felt ready to move.

He describes the shape of his career as '*remarkably linear*'. But perhaps that is the benefit of hindsight. Careers make more sense when they're over.

▶ What has been the shape of your career to date?

▶ How would you describe it?

▶ How far have you gone?

▶ What do you still want to do?

Contrast those first remarks with these by someone about fifteen years younger and, consciously, still in the process of shaping his career.

At times I think it's a very unconventional career, because it's involved a lot of movement, a lot of different organizations across a lot of different sectors. Yet in another way it feels very ordinary, because it has always been in organizations, and I have become progressively more senior, earning more money and doing more managerial work. Actually I still don't think I have a very clear idea what a career is. For a start I don't think you can have much sense of your career until you've spent some time in it. Whatever it is! I think careers are defined retrospectively. You make sense of where you've been. Also your past does, to some extent, define where you can go in the future. But you don't just wait for it to happen. You're constantly redefining the track that you're on to make sense of where you are, where you're coming from, and where you're going. In that sense a career is just a good story that you develop to explain why you're doing what you're doing, both to yourself and to the significant others around you.

A career is a work in progress. One that is defined and redefined over time, and the prime responsibility for doing that is yours. As Erik Erikson [*Identity and the Life Cycle*, Norton, 1980] and other developmental psychologists have shown, we need our work, and in the last resort our lives, to feel meaningful. That's why you put so much energy into your job. But your career is more important than your job. Jobs belong to the organizations that provide them. (It's easy to check that proposition: look who takes jobs away.) Careers belong to you. Ultimately they are what *you* make them.

▶ So what's the story you tell about your career?

▶ Where have you come from?

▶ Who are you now?

▶ Where are you going?

▶ What is the career that you are making?

Your career belongs to you, but that doesn't mean you have a free hand to define it. Of course not. Circumstances intervene. Employment and employers exert their own pressures. You can hear that in this next extract, from one of the youngest managers ever to reach the most senior executive grade in one of the country's largest industrial concerns. It's a reminder that career progression is not a smooth process even for fast-trackers.

I tend to talk about climbing and mountains, or rock scrambling, when I think of my career pattern. I also talk about in at the deep end when describing the transitions I've made from job to job. The climb has been quite steep, but the rate of climb has slowed over the last two years. Now is about my first taste of a z-shaped career experience. I'm considering the options for me now, considering how sharp an incline I should be going for.

Climbs. Inclines. Rocks. Bends in the track. Bumps on the road. It's not plain sailing, not all upward movement, even for those with a history of fast-tracking. No wonder the once-favoured metaphor of the 'career ladder' has fallen into disrepute.

▶ How would you draw or picture your career progress to date?

▶ What obstacles have you encountered and overcome?

▶ How would you describe your current rate of progress?

▶ What obstacles are you facing now?

Career progress can rocket, slow down, or even slam into reverse, an especially hard experience for those accustomed to being fast-trackers.

At age nine, I was the youngest player to represent my school in the football team. At fourteen I was the youngest to play for the under-eighteens. I was the fastest to get a brown belt in karate. At twenty-eight I was the youngest manager in the company and later, when I was head-hunted, at thirty-two I was very young to be part of a management buy-out. I drove myself forward, plateaued for a while, had another mini-launch and progressed rapidly again, then settled, then shot forward again. The metaphor would be something like the eventual launch of a rocket, with a long near perfect ascent, followed by the crash. Probably because company politics finally skewered me while I was in a niche business, so while flying very high and heading higher I was also vulnerable and isolated and unable to be saved.

Here is an important reminder. Careers are competitive. They do not take place in a human vacuum. Organizations are political places. Careers unfold in competitive environments. The interpersonal dimension is a pivotal element in any career equation.

▶ What is the biggest setback that you have experienced in your career?

▶ To what extent did you bring it on yourself?

▶ What particular relationships are important to your continuing career progress?

▶ How skilful and influential are you in relating to these people?

Nor are the ups and downs all to do with other people. Here's another insight. Your priorities, and you, can change as you go through your career. Here is someone who was an early career high-flier in the armed services before she went on to become a senior executive.

My career? It's been a series of stages. Stop–start. My twenties were about establishing my career, but then about getting married and having a family. My thirties were about re-establishing my career, going back in after my marriage broke down. My forties were very much about personal development. Now that I'm in my fifties it's about deploying all the skills and experience that I've gathered to help other people to resource themselves. I've paid more attention to it at certain times, such as when I was first establishing it, and then, as a single parent, having previously resigned my commission, when I was re-establishing it. That meant re-training for a civilian career, which I did by borrowing the money to get the necessary qualification. I went back to work carrying a debt equivalent to my first year's salary. After that I just concentrated on doing a job and consolidating for a while. I did a series of similar jobs in different organizations. There was a common core in each of them. Each brought new challenges, most recently the international dimension. But now I've taken charge of my career again.

▶ What distinct stages can you discern in your career to date?

▶ When has your career *not* been at the front of your mind?

▶ What is prompting you to read this book now?

▶ What else are you doing to take charge of your career?

Sometimes you feel in control of your career. At other times you don't. Often people pay more attention to the job in hand and less to the longer-term career of which it is a part. Also some career domains are naturally slower than others. Here's someone whose career started in education, progressing unusually quickly to senior lecturer, and then took off when he shifted, first into a corporate job and then into independent consultancy.

It was a slow start. I wasted far too long, eleven years, in the education sector but since then it has been upward, rising quite rapidly. It's been like a water-powered roller-coaster that suddenly developed rocket power and then went into free-fall, until the booster rockets came in. I'm not actually in the roller-coaster car, I'm tied to the front like Captain Ahab on Moby Dick.

▶ What's the pace of the career track in your domain?

▶ Which lane are you in? Fast? Slow? Off-road? Don't know?

▶ How urgent are you feeling?

▶ To what extent do you feel in control of your career?

What can we learn from reviewing the experience of careering? Brochures and advertisements might offer smooth progression, but the career track does not provide it. Far from it.

● Careers go through phases.

● The track is seldom clearly defined.

● The experience includes ups and downs.

● Your career is not always at the front of your mind.

● The pace varies.

● Your career is not entirely within your own control.

All careers have turning points, not just the obvious ones such as changes of job or organization, but more subtle, more frequent and potentially more significant twists and turns wound into the fabric of careering along. That's part of the nature of the track. It includes 'hotspots' and we will have much more to say about them.

But before we get into the detail, are there some broader insights that you can take away from reviewing the experience of careering? What are the big factors that govern the pace of the career track? And what can you do to control them?

Controlling the pace

If you ask people what determined the pace of their career progress, you will get a rich variety of answers. Here's a few that I've collected. Each cluster is one individual's answer. Some people offer more reasons than others.

- *The ability to see the way forward.*

- *Recognizing the dangers from competitors, external or internal.*

- *A mentor.*

- *Time to think. (Long-haul flights are especially useful.)*

- *Thinking strategies and frameworks. (These have helped me to think on my feet.)*

- *Self-awareness.*

- *Divine providence. Good fortune. External events.*

- *Being ready to move to the front-line elsewhere. (Being single pays in this respect.)*

- *Having a good IQ, meaning I could adapt to new circumstances fairly quickly.*

- *Opportunities arising on a regular basis.*

- *Me being flexible.*

- *Achieving a track record.*

- *Having a reputation for learning quickly.*

- *Working initially in a very small company ... It gave me breadth and access that I wouldn't have got in a bigger organization.*

- *Someone to talk to and to help you make sense of your opportunities.*

- *An ability on your own part to create opportunities. That's partly being open-minded about what might come out of an opportunity situation, and partly skills, like being able to build good relationships.*

- *Having good communications with head-hunters.*

- *A preparedness to move around and take some risks, including suffering some personal inconvenience, both for yourself and for your significant others. You put a lot of time into a career, so it entails making sacrifices in other parts of your life.*

- *Being an efficient learner. Extracting the learning from your experiences.*

- *Branding. It also helps to work for well-known brands. It makes people interested in you and prepared to talk to you. There is still something rather superficial about how people get opportunities to move between organiza-tions. External recruitment relies on some fairly crude indicators, such as whether you've been to the right institution, and whether you've been at big name businesses, and whether you have had the right 'experiences', like 'turn-round' or 'mergers and acquisition'.*

Clearly experiences differ. Individuals attribute their progress to different factors or combinations of factors. But is there any pattern in all of this? I believe so.

Here's the proposition …

Capability matters.
But so does opportunity.
And visibility.
And credibility.
And therefore other people.

Capability, opportunity, visibility, credibility, other people. These are the core factors that govern the pace of your career progress.

Career progression is only partly to do with your abilities. They are very important, but they are far from the whole story, as experience again demonstrates.

Opportunity matters.

A half-chance role to answer phones for three weeks became a ten-year career worth nearly a million.

But opportunities are not straightforward.
Throughout my career I have always remembered some advice from my karate teacher, 'you have to recognize opportunities before you can take them'.

You can get opportunities wrong.
It's not just the loss of time, it's also the problem of explaining it, that flows from making a bad choice of job.

And other people often control access to opportunities, quite independently of your talents and capabilities.
At times you could choose what you were going to do next, but these times were not frequent.

Visibility matters. You need to be noticed.
There was a slow phase when I was lost as a junior brand manager. I emerged from this one by running a rather good televised promotion by myself, which gave me great visibility within the company.

Or you need to make yourself noticed.
The people who really wanted to get on would pester and badger and cajole the Resourcing Manager to assign them to high-profile projects.

Bad work will raise your visibility too, but it won't help your career prospects!

Visibility is not the same as capability or even opportunity. It is a distinct ingredient in career progression.
My break came when the company instituted a one-year research scholarship at one of the universities. I think they expected all the applications to come from technical people, but I applied to do research into industrial relations. I didn't get the scholarship. I don't even think my proposal was particularly well put together. But it attracted some high-level interest and after that my name stayed on headquarters' radar.

Visibility is important, especially early on. But once you're visible the determining factor becomes credibility.

So credibility matters. But reputations are often founded on limited evidence. Repute can run ahead of reality. So you need reputation sustained over time. Once again this should – and usually does – have a great deal to do with your capabilities. But yet again there can be more to it than that. Such as the eyes of the significant beholders, the judges of performance and gatekeepers of career opportunities.

The eye of the beholder may be fair …
For me the star is the person who takes a problem away and takes account- ability for it.

Or the eye may be idiosyncratic, biased, or just plain unreasonable …
You're clearly not committed, because you've not had a divorce yet.

If opportunity, visibility and credibility matter, then other people matter. They may or may not influence your personal capabilities as such, but they will certainly affect your prospects for career progression.

So here's your challenge. Of these five factors the one most obviously with- in your own control, arguably the only one directly within your control, is capability. But the extent and rate of your career progress are going to depend on more than just your capabilities. Progress depends on capability *plus* opportunity *plus* visibility *plus* credibility. Much therefore depends on other people, whether they see you and what they think of you when they do.

So the vital question for you becomes, which capabilities generate the most opportunities, the most visibility and the most credibility? There are so many capabilities that you might develop. Most organizations these days have long lists of desirable characteristics in their competency frameworks, candidate specifications and assessment criteria. But you can't concentrate on everything. What's the secret? Which capabilities should you focus on developing so as to accelerate your career to the next stage and to perform successfully when you get there?

The answer is in the chapters that follow, in The Fast Track Formula.

Where next?

We live our careers individually, uniquely, gradually. That makes it difficult for anyone to discern a guiding pattern in advance. On the surface careers vary enormously. But beneath this apparent variety there is a deeper similarity, a hidden structure that is common to all occupational domains. Understanding that structure is the basis for having a rapid grasp of context, the first of the capabilities that make up the Fast Track Formula.

2

CHAPTER TWO

The Hidden Structure
of Careers

A mysterious parcel

Your career is a mysterious parcel. Addressed to you, but heavily wrapped. Nor does it come pre-assembled. You have to unwrap each of the parts in turn and figure out how they fit. You have to put it together for yourself. Construction plans are not provided. The piece in hand demands your concentration. The whole process takes time.

Consequently, it is difficult to see what is coming next or how to prepare for the next phase. That is why so many careers falter and fail. You move into a new role and it turns out to be not only different from what you had expected but much more difficult. One of the paradoxes of career progression is this. Doing well in one level of work will tend to get you promoted to the next. But the characteristics, which previously enabled you to do well, are not the ones that are now critically important for success at the new level.

Part of the problem comes from being wrapped up yourself, immersed in your more immediate concerns. It is hard to make out the shape of the future as you career along in real time, living your career in close-up. In close-up you focus on the details and specifics of the task in hand. In terms of doing a good job and keeping yourself in contention for progression, that's necessary. You won't get far if you neglect the day job. But it's not an either/or choice. To steer and accelerate your career, you also need to pay attention to the broader pattern of work. You need to know in advance about how the nature of work will change as you progress into the higher levels of your career.

Work changes markedly at the different levels in virtually every occupation. Progressing upwards over the course of your career, you will find yourself faced with very different types of challenge. Unfortunately, the words used to describe career progression do little to prepare you. The language is fuzzy. We talk of jobs becoming 'bigger' or 'more senior'. We talk of 'being promoted' or 'career advancement'. We talk of wanting 'greater challenge'. But all these expressions are vague. What do they actually mean? What is really involved in moving upward?

This chapter peels away these wrappings so that you can see the hidden structure of careers. Then you will know what to expect and can gain an edge by preparing yourself for the next level of challenge.

The changing nature of work

What is the hidden structure? The voices of experience again provide some insights. Let's hear a couple of senior managers describing how the nature of their work changed over the course of their careers.

Here's the first.

It changed in many ways. Obviously one spent more time managing other people and much less doing actual marketing work. Doing became showing. There was a lot of time setting targets, planning, checking, motivating, integrating and training.

Interpersonal skills became increasingly important.

Initiative became vital; the ability to self-start, self-correct, and generally control one's agenda.

Also, increasing time and effort was spent on ceremonial functions (particularly working overseas), pressing the flesh, paying visits to the front, preaching the gospel.

Naturally the focus of one's time horizon became quite a long way ahead. I spent a lot more of my time on justice matters; fair distribution of resources and rewards, separating squabbling team members, and redirecting effort to the market and to the opponents.

The second is even more distilled, making the underlying pattern still clearer.

There is less doing and more thinking, leading and directing. You switch from leading through personal contact to leading by providing the right framework, leadership and team. I think there have been three phases. First, learning how to do things. Secondly, learning how to get things done through other people. And thirdly, learning how to get things done through other people you may not even meet. You need a different skill-set for each stage.

These examples are both managerial. But you get a similar story in virtually any other occupational domain.

Ask a public relations professional …

There are definite levels. When you start, say in the Press Office, you're responsible for basic work like compiling the press cuttings and circulating them, for managing the magazine library, sorting and keeping cuttings, and other mundane tasks like organizing the complimentary diaries and Christmas cards. In the PR office you cut your teeth on local stories with the local press, essentially descriptive stuff.

You know you've gone up a level when you're allowed to handle trade press and public relations issues that are potentially more controversial, where what you say needs to be more carefully attuned to company policies. And at the top end, Director of Corporate Communications, or whatever it is called, the work is more political than anything. You spend your time dealing with, often pre-handling, major issues with the national media and between the organization's stakeholders that might have an impact on the media. You spend a lot of time working to make sure people are all pointing in the same direction on a subject.

Ask a librarian …

The roles are just qualitatively different at different stages in the career hierarchy. You start off stamping the books that are being issued and shelving the ones that have been returned. And procedures don't get much more clearly defined than that. Basically that's all our Saturday girls do. In middle-ranking jobs, where most of the professionals are, your job is about exploiting the library's resources. Thinking about things like what stock to hold and how to make the best use of this year's book fund budget, and answering non-routine queries from the public. Then when you get into the top jobs, and there aren't many of them, you're into deciding matters like where will we have libraries in the future and what will they look like? How will we utilize new technologies? How are patterns of need and interest for publicly available information changing and how are we going to respond to that? You will be consulted about those things, when you're in a middle-level role, but you know that it won't be your decision.

Ask an airline pilot ...

What's the difference between co-pilot and captain? The co-pilot does more flying so that the pilot can be freed up to do more thinking. There are simply more demands to think on the captain. You start off with an agenda to get safely from A to B and you're working through your procedures for departure when, for instance, your Cabin Services Director comes in with an issue about a passenger who's pressing to be upgraded from club class to first. You need to be able to prioritize your different agendas. You've always got to be thinking about your duty of care to your passengers, your obligations as a licence holder and your responsibilities as an employee of the airline. Going on to become a Training Captain is another big step. You can't just teach the answers, because the pilot's job is to make judgements. What you have to do is to create a culture and instil a questioning instinct. The essence of it is to get them into the habit of thinking ahead and anticipating problems before they arise. And the most difficult bit is for pilots to learn to monitor and give themselves feedback so that their approach is slick but not rushed. A lot of the Training Captain's work is role-modelling. In the old days the Captain was a god-like figure who wore white gloves. Nowadays they are communicators, co-ordinating teams and multiple demands: operational, business, customer, legal, technical, organizational and political. You have to create that.

Check out other examples for yourself: consultancy, banking, teaching, advertising, policing, accountancy, publishing, whatever. Call a friend. Ask a practitioner. There is a qualitative shift in the nature of the work to be done at different stages in any career. Observe the people working at higher levels in your own domain, whatever that may be. It will give you a glimpse of your future.

These first-hand insights give us some strong indications about how the nature of work changes. They also show that careers can readily be distinguished – at least after the event – into three broad categories of lower-, middle- and higher-level activities. However, in all these descriptions, the surface features, the particulars of each case, still partially obscure the essence of the underlying structure.

Not for long.

A new view of the pyramid

Fortunately, a few people have studied levels of work closely. Among them organizational researchers Elliott Jaques and Gillian Stamp, of Brunel University's Institute of Organization and Social Studies, have explored, articulated and developed what they call 'stratified systems theory'. Don't be put off by its awesome-sounding title. The concept clarifies the essence of what is involved at different 'levels of work'.

Jaques has identified seven distinct levels of work, ranging from the most basic to the realms of world-leadership. We're not going to examine all seven levels here. To clarify the nature of career progression, it is sufficient to simplify the concept into lower-, middle- and higher-level roles. These three big chunks are easier to recognize and to keep in mind.

Bear in mind that these labels – lower, middle and higher – are not judgements about you or your worth or potential. They are simply a way of making some important distinctions about how the nature of work changes. How quickly you find yourself in the middle and higher levels depends on how fast your career is tracking.

As you read these descriptions, think about what level of work you are currently engaged in. Think carefully. Job titles are notoriously unreliable guides to the true level of work. They are often just another part of the wrapping that makes it difficult for you to see where the real qualitative shifts occur.

- Lower-level work is essentially about delivery and service.

- Middle-level work is about co-ordination and management.

- Higher-level work is about definition and direction.

You need different capabilities for each. So, as the critical requirements for each level are outlined, make a note of any that you personally need to develop.

Lower-level roles

Lower-level roles are essentially hands-on. Here you are expected to have the know-how required to get the job done personally, directly. Work at this level is comparatively well-defined, governed by rules, or at least by established standards, if not written procedures. This limits the discretion with which acceptable work can be done. Of course there is a requirement to think, but it is relatively constrained. This is the realm of right and wrong answers. This work does not require sophisticated interpersonal skills. A basic, even an inconsistent level, of politeness and communication skill will suffice. Because regulations and procedures call for a particular type of response to a particular type of problem, then essentially it is conditioning and training, rather than free-thinking or interpersonal sensitivity, that are required.

What capabilities do you need to perform effectively in lower-level work? You will be judged to have performed successfully at this level, if you follow the procedures, do what is expected and produce prompt service and timely delivery. So what do you need to do?

- Get things done, as expected.

- Be reliable, dependable and conscientious.

- Conform, fix non-conformities by following the rules and highlight them if you can't fix them.

- Be more than averagely productive.

- Be energetic.

- Provide speed of response.

- Be eager to please.

Do you have these capabilities?

They are all useful. They will help you to do effective lower-level work. That will give you visibility and credibility with the powers that be. And that in turn will tend to get you promoted. Some of these things will continue to be useful. But they aren't the critical capabilities for the next level of work.

If you rely on lower-level attributes in middle-level roles, you won't get very far because you'll be perceived as a doer rather than an organizer, a person who can only apply the rules rather than interpret them, someone who firefights rather than manages.

Here's why ...

Middle-level roles

Middle-level roles are more complex. They require you to be able to handle more variables. Work at this level entails thinking through competing demands and priorities, facing up to dilemmas and having to make judgement calls of a sort that are not required in lower-level work. This is a greyer, less black-and-white, less well-defined territory. Middle-level work is about setting priorities for what is done at the lower level or resolving problems referred up from there. The thinking challenge has become greater. You are no longer in the realm of right and wrong answers. Work now requires a higher level of critical thinking. It demands more evaluative thought, more consideration of possible causes and prospective consequences, both the immediate ones and the subsequent repercussions.

The interpersonal challenge has likewise become more demanding. The need to make decisions about how resources are – and are not – allocated, introduces a political dimension that has been much less conspicuous up to this point. Lower-level work may include some lobbying and politicking, pressing for resources and for agreement. But middle-level work is more complex, because it involves being on the receiving end, as well as in the middle, of those activities and at the same time having to maintain effective working relationships. Whether or not these roles include responsibility for managing others, the middle is the level where policies and intentions need to be translated into tasks and actions, not simply through one's own direct actions, but indirectly through other people.

What capabilities do you need to perform effectively in middle-level work? How will you be judged to have done well at this level? Through providing linkage, by co-ordinating and managing the work of others. What do you need to do here?

- Recognize competing demands.

- Resolve conflicts.

- Make decisions with reference to business policies and priorities.

- Co-ordinate, facilitate and develop the work of others.

- Do the planning to turn intentions into practice.

- Allocate scarce resources efficiently.

- Make judgements that turn out to be balanced and sound.

- Maintain working relationships despite having to disagree with people on occasions.

Do you have *these* capabilities?

Again they are all useful. They will help you to do effective middle-level work. That will give you visibility and credibility with the people above you. And that might get you promoted. But these aren't the critical capabilities for higher-level work.

If you simply demonstrate middle-level attributes, you probably won't get into higher-level work, and if you do, you'll have to learn quickly. Otherwise you'll be seen as a fixer rather than a strategist, someone who can interpret rules but not someone who can redefine them in the first place, as an enabler rather than a leader.

Here's why ...

Higher-level roles

Higher-level roles are more complex still. This is the level of work where the focus shifts from the present to the future and from the internal to the external. More exactly, this is where the focus must include, and continue to shift between, the future and the present, the external and the internal. This is where work becomes strategic. At this level it is not sufficient to be concerned solely with current practice or with merely extrapolating from existing precedents. Nor is it sufficient to confine your attention to what is happening within the narrowly defined boundaries of the particular organization or occupational domain in which you happen to be working. All the systems in which careers are located – organizations, professions, occupations – are affected by what happens, and emerges over time, in the wider social, technological, economic, political and competitive environments. Working at the higher level requires you to attend to the trends and developments in these environments. Consequently, the range of factors that you may need to consider and integrate increases dramatically. And again the shift is not merely quantitative, but also qualitative. The issues that need to be thought about become, by their nature, more complex, more uncertain, more dynamic than in the previous levels of work.

Although middle-level work is already evaluative, higher-level work is increasingly interpretative, because there is more ambiguity involved. Higher-level work is also highly creative, because it is about shaping as well as responding to emerging futures. And so higher-level work also presents higher-level interpersonal challenges. It requires visions to be developed and implemented, not directly but indirectly, through various others with whom you may never come into direct contact. Consequently, higher-level work entails multiple relationships, a wide variety of differing interests to be considered, frequently diverse people to be persuaded, alliances and coalitions to be formed, nurtured and sustained.

What capabilities do you need to perform effectively in higher-level work? How will you be judged fit for this level, where work itself has become non-routine, fluid, interpretative and creative? In this context the key capabilities are different again, and become harder to define comprehensively. What do you need here?

- Tolerance of uncertainty.
- A continuing awareness and understanding of varied, external, environmental forces.
- An acute sense of possibilities, opportunities as well as problems.
- To make connections between the big picture and the small detail, and vice versa.
- To make sense of complex, uncertain, dynamic and ambiguous situations.
- An inquiring frame of mind, actively searching for significance.
- To ask questions and consider multiple perspectives.
- To think through extended 'what if' scenarios.
- To establish new and purposeful directions.
- To devise and articulate multidimensional strategies and intentions.
- A combination of creativity and realism.
- To make ideas and concepts accessible and inspiring for others.
- The trustworthiness to mobilize coalitions of diverse interest groups.
- To persuade others to pursue propositions that are not yet proven.

Without these capabilities you will ultimately be seen as lightweight. Do you have them yet? Do others accept that you have them?

If not, read on.

The accelerators

Even simplifying careers into three broad phases produces a daunting list of capabilities that are going to be needed. That's not surprising, because work becomes a complex business. But there is a thread that runs through this story. Or more precisely three. And they will give you a grip on what it is that you need to do. So let's stand back from the detail. Instead compare and contrast the two ends of a career, the low and the high. It's a good way of drawing out distinctions that otherwise go unnoticed. In this case it highlights the key capabilities required for career progression.

Jobs at the bottom are usually simpler, more straightforward.
Jobs at the top tend to be more complex.

Jobs at the bottom are often quite repetitive and routine.
Jobs at the top usually have more variety and less predictability.

Jobs at the bottom are generally well-defined, usually by someone else.
Jobs at the top have more scope for the job-holder to define them.

Work at the bottom usually has considerable clarity.
Work at the top often involves much uncertainty.

Jobs at the bottom usually have quite a close time horizon; the focus is relatively short-term.
Jobs at the top have longer-term time horizons.

Jobs at the bottom often involve working with other people.
So do jobs at the top.
No difference there, then. Or is there?

Jobs at the bottom can involve working with a lot of people, but often in quite a specific, brief or well-defined way.
Jobs at the top often involve working with a lot of people, usually in a more extensive, ongoing and less prescribed way.

Jobs at the bottom don't usually involve having to manage other people.
Jobs at the top usually do.

Work at the bottom means doing it yourself.
Work at the top means other people doing lots of things for you.

Work at the bottom means a narrower range of responsibility.
Work at the top means a much broader range of responsibility.

Work at the bottom may involve making decisions, but there are usually guidelines, policies or rules to help you do that, and the impact of these decisions is relatively limited.
Work at the top certainly involves making decisions, and the impact of these decisions can be much greater.

Work at the bottom means you can have a direct impact on the things that you are expected to do.
Work at the top means that you have to achieve lots of things indirectly, by relying on other people
And relying on other people isn't always a very comfortable feeling.

Work at the bottom is close to the action; you can see the effect of your actions almost immediately, and hear about it from others pretty quickly when something goes wrong.
Work at the top can be a long way from the action; it can take a long time to realize what's going on, especially as the information may have to come through so many people to get to you.
And maybe they modify the story, deliberately or otherwise, *en route*.

Work at the bottom carries less expectation to think creatively.
Work at the top is expected to be more strategic, more creative.

Work at the bottom is about implementing directions; it can be reactive.
Work at the top is about deciding direction; it needs to be more proactive.

Once you look at the overall shape of career progression in this way, the hidden structure becomes clear.

The context changes, becoming

- Broader in scope and longer in time

- More complex

- Less clearly defined

- More dynamic

- More unpredictable.

What you have to think about changes, becoming

- More varied
- More complicated
- More uncertain
- More left to your own discretion
- More mentally demanding.

How you have to work with other people changes, becoming

- More political
- More significant in its consequences
- More subject to negotiation
- More indirect
- More interpersonally challenging.

Look again at the first-hand examples near the beginning of this chapter. You'll find that it is now much easier to see these three threads, now that you know they're there.

Your grasp of context, your thinking capability and the quality of your interaction with others – these are the real career accelerators. These are the three key capabilities that constitute the fast track formula, because each successive stage of career progression demands higher-order performance in each of these three respects.

These are the real accelerators because they connect one level of work to the next. These are the three capabilities that directly address the three principal challenges that escalate over the course of a career. Developing these capabilities therefore equips you not only for the long gradient of the career track, for its gradual, shifting inclines, but also for its sudden twists and turns. Developing these capabilities means that future prospects and immediate performance are both well served.

This is because you need the same three capabilities in the hotspots, in those episodes at work when your mettle is being tested. When you are up against it, when your competence is being tried, when your performance is being judged. In these moments, this know-how – that grasp of context, quality of thinking and quality of interaction – are key capabilities that can help you to redirect your attention quickly to where it is most needed.

To put it another way, if you recognize where you are, then you can raise your game accordingly.

That is why these first two chapters have focused on giving you a sharper appreciation of context, of the nature of the career track, its sudden bends as well as its gradual inclines. Now you have to judge – and go on judging – the context in which you find yourself. So here are some further nuances to watch out for, as you go.

Understanding your own track

The contours of the track can vary. The distribution of roles across the levels of work varies from one occupation to another. In teaching, for example, most of the jobs are clustered in the middle level with relatively few higher-level roles. In management consultancy, by contrast, a greater proportion of jobs are located in higher-level work.

The speed of the track can vary. The going is slower in some career domains than others. There are faster and slower lanes – and even some off-roading – in the world of work. This is because some domains, such as law, accountancy, financial services, commercial flying, aircraft design, are more closely regulated than others, such as advertising, sales and marketing, tourism, interior design.

The volume of traffic can vary. Some careers are more popular, more crowded, and more competitive, than others. How fast you progress will always depend partly on the sheer number – quite apart from the quality – of other drivers on the track. This is bound to affect opportunity, so the sooner you develop the three fast-track capabilities – to improve your visibility and credibility – the better.

Finally, the track may not be well marked. The changeover from one level of work to the next is not always obvious. Organizations often clutter their hierarchies with jobs doing essentially the same level of work. Job titling can obscure more than it reveals. However, higher-level roles usually continue to include some proportion of lower-level activities. What you need to do is to extend your thinking and relating capabilities as a matter of priority and to remain sharply aware of context, of when to use particular levels of your repertoire.

Contextual hotspots

Here are three crossroads along the career track at which to be particularly alert. These are very commonly contextual hotspots.

First, when you change job. Whether you change role, organization, sector, level of work, or some combination of these, you will find yourself in transition, a new context with new demands. The more quickly you get a grasp of them, the faster you'll attain fully effective performance and maintain your career momentum.

Secondly, when your boss changes. This is most obviously when one boss moves on and another takes over. Less obviously it is when your existing boss remains but their role expands or changes, or they start to do higher-level work. Either way, you are likely to find yourself in a new context, with changes in the way you are perceived and the expectations that are held of you. Another contextual hotspot.

Thirdly, in a reorganization. Reorganization has become a condition rather than an event in many sectors. Clearly, it can precipitate the previous two types of contextual hotspot, changes in your boss or in your own role. But reorganization is also a category in its own right, because it usually produces broader contextual changes that will also affect your career progression. Reorganization may mean new judges and gatekeepers, new patterns of visibility and credibility, new cultural norms and expectations, new rules of the game. It is a prime situation, therefore, in which you need to be able to get a rapid grasp of context.

Where next?

Career progression will take you into qualitatively different contexts. Higher-level roles make higher-order demands, both mental and interpersonal. The capabilities of higher-order thinking and relating produce not only higher-order performance but also a reliable basis for continuing career progression. So it is to those capabilities that we turn next, starting with the development of higher-order thinking.

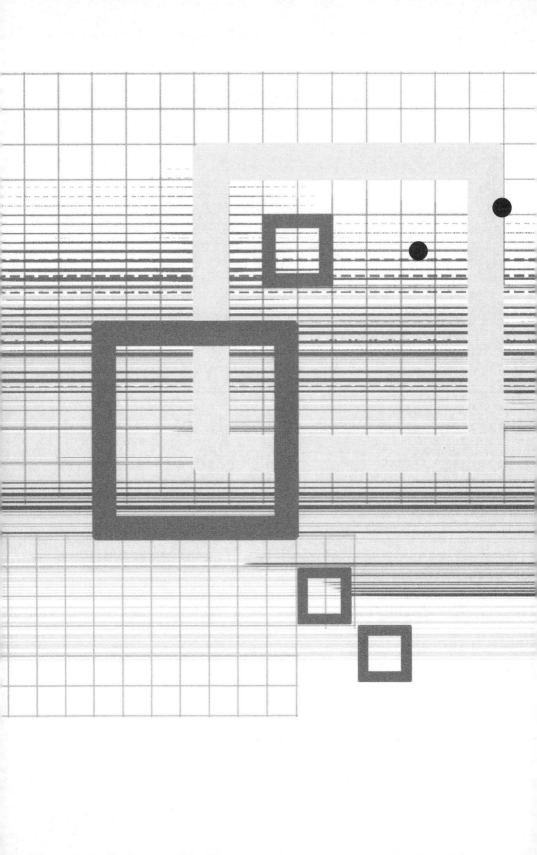

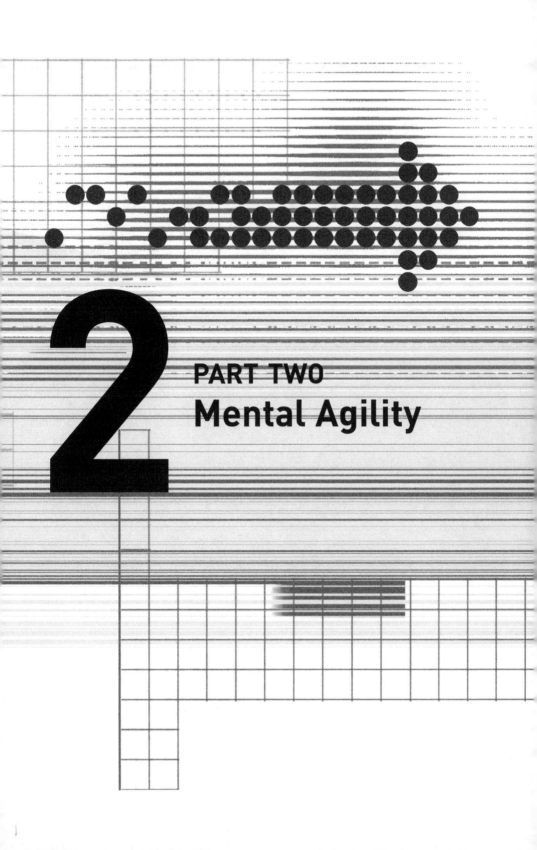

2

PART TWO
Mental Agility

3

CHAPTER THREE

Higher-Order Thinking (HOT Stuff)

Thinking at the edge

What's on your mind?

It's an important question. This chapter is designed to help you to develop the higher-order thinking capabilities required to do higher-order jobs. Doing that successfully is based on recognizing the nature of the thinking challenges that face you, both currently and in the foreseeable future. It also needs some insight into the character of your thinking, the way you tend to use your mind now.

What's on your mind now? The things that stick in our minds tend to be the ones that we are having difficulty processing. Problems we struggle to resolve. Opportunities we can't quite decide about. Challenges that are multifaceted, that shift and change and are hard to figure through. This is thinking at the edge, and it is where we stand to do our most valuable work. If you want your career to progress, you need to be able to perform at the edge.

But edges are tricky. The challenges that bring us the greatest visibility and credibility, when we handle them successfully, are also the ones most likely to expose the edge of our capabilities, and to tip us over the edge of our confidence.

We need to be able to see all these edges. The tricky angles of our work, stuff that needs to be thought through carefully. The shape of our thinking, habits of mind that can limit the way we approach important mental challenges. And the edge of our self-belief, which may or may not be accurately aligned with the challenges of the situation. In one respect, at least, climbing upwards in a career is exactly like finding your way up a mountain. It's dangerous to rush at it mindlessly.

So, let's go at it mindfully, taking a closer look at what's on *your* mind.

Your current thinking challenges

You are going to be presented with a series of reflective exercises, thinking tasks. My strong advice is that you don't just skip read through them. If you're serious about developing higher-order thinking capabilities, you need to be prepared to look hard at how you think now. And the best way to get a realistic picture of that is to focus on the issues that pre-occupy you.

So, when you think about your work, what is uppermost in your mind right now? Think about it! Make a short list. The things that are currently on your mind. Write them down somewhere.

-

-

-

Now, think about the nature of the thinking challenge that these issues present. To help you do that, here are a number of scales, describing various qualities. In each case the opposite ends of the spectrum have been named. Consider your issue in relation to the first scale and mark where you think it lies on that particular dimension. Then go through the same process for each of the other scales in turn. This will build up a picture of the nature of the challenge.

- -

familiar   unfamiliar

- -

simple   complex

- -

clearly-defined   loosely-defined

----

short-term task   long-term project

----

a fixed target   a moving target

----

routine   innovative

----

predictable outcomes   unpredictable

----

a hands-on task   a hands-off task

----

in own control   need others' buy-in

----

tangible outcomes   intangible outcomes

----

physical   conceptual

----

feedback easy to get   feedback hard to get

Go through the same exercise with each of the issues that are on your mind before you proceed to interpret your scores.

Now sit back and look at the patterns that have emerged. Start with your biggest issue, the challenge that is uppermost in your mind. Look at the overall shape of your assessment of that issue. The further, and the more frequently, it falls towards the right of these scales, the more the issue exhibits the characteristics of a higher-order thinking challenge. And the more it needs you to apply higher-order thinking capabilities to tackle it.

An issue does not need to score towards the right-hand end of all of the scales to constitute a HOT (higher-order thinking) challenge. HOT challenges can be multidimensional. The reason for using several scales is to improve the prospects of recognizing a higher-order thinking challenge and appreciating the nature of what you are up against.

Nor do you need to worry about the accuracy of your scaling. Work does vary in its level of complexity, uncertainty, ambiguity, but the purpose of this exercise is to measure the challenge facing you personally, not to assess the work as such. The important question is how the challenge seems to you, since it's your mind that has to grapple with it.

There is, however, one important distinction that you do need to make. Often an issue is at the front of our minds simply because it is urgent. This does not make it unimportant. But equally it does not, in itself, make it a higher-order thinking challenge. If an issue is urgent, but essentially familiar, routine, within your control and so on, then just get on with it. Don't invest in unnecessarily elaborate thinking about it. That is a waste of mental energy. It may also be a form of prevarication or avoidance, which may be a pointer to some other sort of anxiety on your part, often to do with someone else and the reaction that you anticipate, and perhaps fear, on their part. This might be to do with timeliness, cost, quality of service, whatever. But it is essentially a challenge for your interpersonal skills rather than your thinking capabilities. We'll come to the art of influential relating in Part Three. That's an element in the fast track formula in its own right.

However, an issue may be *both* urgent *and* a higher-order mental challenge. You may well have issues of this sort. In that case, you need certainly to think before you act. And you need to think well.

Is your thinking up to it?

Before providing you with a framework to enable you to arrive at an informed and objective answer to this question, there are myths to be exploded. First, discard the myth that how well someone can think is essentially predetermined by the cards that nature dealt. By the size, speed and capacity of the brain tissue carried inside that particular cranium. Secondly, discard the related myth that how well someone thinks, and consequently their potential for senior roles, can be reliably predicted from how they perform on multiple choice 'intelligence' tests. This is a myth to which too many people, employers and individuals alike, still subscribe. The consequence of both misconceptions is to limit career opportunities, personal development and career progress.

The endurance of these misunderstandings is particularly negligent, since the nature – and, more importantly, the develop-ability – of good thinking have been deeply researched over the last twenty years. Prominent contributions to this work have been made by Harvard cognitive researcher, David Perkins, who illuminates the issues clearly in his book, *Outsmarting IQ: the emerging science of learnable intelligence* [Free Press, 1995].

Perkins distinguishes three types of intelligence, three facets of mental power. First, there is neural intelligence, the speed and efficiency of thinking and reasoning which comes from the neurophysiology of your particular brain. This is the hard-wiring. Not much you can do about that. You get the skull you are given. This is relevant to how well you think, but it is only one part of the story.

Secondly, there is experiential intelligence, what you put into that skull along the way. This is your accumulated learning, know-how, expertise, domain knowledge, call it what you will. Clearly, there is a lot that you can do about that. It is a major element of your thinking capability, particularly given that we don't just think, we think about particular things. So knowledge about those things, how they work and how they can be influenced, is hugely relevant.

But there are a couple of snags with experiential intelligence. One is that it takes time to acquire expertise. The time required to accumulate know-how is always going to be a constraint on fast-tracking. Another snag is that experiential intelligence is double-edged. It prompts us to see things in particular ways, through the lens of the particular knowledge and expertise that we have accumulated. Like any other framework it will both highlight and limit. We work and learn in particular contexts and, consequently, our learning and know-how can become context-specific. This is one of the things that can make life difficult when, as it does, the career context changes.

So experiential intelligence needs to be used with care. When we use it, we need to be mindful of what we're doing. Otherwise it can mislead.

All of this makes the third element of mental power particularly important. This is what Perkins calls reflective intelligence, essentially thinking about thinking. The technical term is *meta-cognition*, which means monitoring how we think and managing our own thinking in a deliberate, mindful way. This is the facet of intelligence over which we have most control. It is also the most learnable. And that makes it highly relevant for anyone who wants to accelerate their career progression, to rise to the demands that come with higher-order thinking challenges.

At the heart of reflective intelligence are our thinking 'dispositions'. The concept has been developed by David Perkins and his Harvard colleagues Shari Tishman and Eileen Jay, and parallels have been put forward by other researchers into cognition, suggesting that the concept is robust. Thinking dispositions describe the manner or personality of our thinking. The concept is richer, and more relevant to what actually happens in practice, than the narrower concept of mental ability. After all, we probably all know people who score highly on tests of reasoning or intelligence, but who do not seem to use this ability in practice. This is because, as the phrase 'thinking disposition' suggests, effective thinking involves more than just ability. It also requires inclination, the tendency to think in particular ways. This is particularly important, since tendency is partly a matter of motivation – we like to do it – and partly one of sensitivity – we recognize when to do it.

And 'recognizing when' is the essence of the fast track formula. All its elements – a rapid grasp of context, a quick appreciation of thinking challenge, a facility for relating in the interactive moment – are developments of this theme. That's why we keep coming back to the importance of recognizing the hotspot. Again and again. And that is why thinking dispositions are pivotal not only to higher-order thinking, but to the whole challenge of accelerating your career.

So, let's give you a means of assessing your own thinking dispositions, and then we'll look at them and how to develop them in more detail.

How do you think?

The most direct way to get some insight into this question is to come back to the present, the things that are occupying your thoughts. Think about an important project or objective that you are pursuing now. A project that is real and current. It might be one that is already up and running, or one that you are in the process of launching. Focus on something that feels significant for you. Probably something that you can't achieve single-handedly. Something a level more complex than that. Something that will test your higher-order thinking.

It might be a piece of new business that you want to win. Perhaps it's about securing support for an idea or proposal that you're developing. Or maybe you're involved in some planning that you want to influence towards a particular outcome.

Whatever it is, I'll provide a series of generic questions to help you collect your thoughts.

- What is your project or objective?

- What are you trying to achieve?

Okay, now think about a forthcoming *episode* in that project. I know that makes it sound a bit like an excerpt from a television drama serial, but our occupational lives are not so very different from that. They usually have some sort of weekly pattern, much of what goes on is mundane, and they are punctuated by occasional dramas of one size or another.

Your forthcoming episode may well be a meeting that you need to have with other people. Perhaps it's a presentation or a review or a negotiation of some sort. Much of work involves negotiation, even if it isn't labelled as such. Whatever it is, 'forthcoming' is the key word.

- What exactly is your forthcoming episode?

- Who else is involved?

- What's the purpose of the encounter?

- What's to be discussed?

- What is at stake?

Once you've reminded, note *re-minded*, yourself about the specific context in this way, have a closer look at your thinking by asking yourself some further questions. The objective is to go beyond *what* you are thinking about, to get a sense of *how* you are thinking about it. How you do your thinking. How you keep your mind's eye on it. How you steer that thinking.

Incidentally, you may be concerned that relying on self-report will distort the findings of this exercise. But you're not being assessed for a job here. At least not by anyone else. This is to give you greater self-awareness. The person who has best access to the data is you. The person who stands to gain most from examining this data objectively is also you.

So, over to you. I suggest you take some time over this. Writing yourself some notes is also helpful because it slows the process down a bit. It makes it easier to catch your thoughts. Pinning them down on a piece of paper gives you a better look at them, and also more time to think about your manner of thinking them.

So, it's time to put the coffee on. Or maybe to fetch the bottle-opener. I hope you've made yourself comfortable. Here are the prompting questions. Read them through first to get your mind working on them. Then attend to them one at a time.

- How are you feeling about this forthcoming encounter?

- What's important about it?

- What's challenging about it?

- What aspects of it are going to be most difficult?

- What are you concentrating on?

- How are you doing that?

- How are you organizing your thoughts?

- How would you describe the way you are thinking?

- How are you directing or steering your thinking?

- In what directions are you taking it? Why?

The questions in the second half of the list may be harder to quarry. But, if you persevere, they yield a richer sort of answer. They give us some clues about your thinking dispositions. So, what have you got?

You are looking for two sorts of clue. Most importantly, you are looking for indications of the higher-order thinking dispositions. We'll come to those in a moment. Often more immediate, however, are the indications of their absence. Specifically, indications that the manner of your thinking is …

- Hasty

- Narrow

- Fuzzy

- Disorganized.

I'm taking pains not to call these characteristics of 'lower-order' thinking. That is because, in themselves, they do not necessarily represent poor thinking. In many circumstances they constitute perfectly adequate thinking.

For example, when you're dealing with a problem that is very familiar to you. You've encountered it before. You know how to deal with it. You know what will happen. You don't have to think too much about it. Perhaps it's giving an established presentation, or checking a standard letter, or analyzing a regular report. You'll have your own specific examples. In situations like this you can think relatively quickly and narrowly. You don't particularly need to organize your thoughts or take time to make sense of what's going on. You know where you are and you can just get on with it.

In these circumstances it is wasteful to commit mental energy unnecessarily. The human mind likes economy. This is a pretty smart attitude, because the brain makes a disproportionate demand on the rest of the body's energy resources, blood, oxygen and so on. The attitude tends to work, because so much of what we encounter is familiar. This means that, after a while at least, our mental response can be largely automatic. We are creatures of habit because, for the most part, it serves us well to be so.

Consequently, our thinking dispositions tend to have a 'default' setting, which is for our thinking to be …

- Quick (aka 'hasty')

- Along accustomed lines (aka 'narrow')

- Approximate rather than precise (aka 'fuzzy')

- Spontaneous (aka 'disorganized').

Do you see the relevance for career progression? Patterns of thinking – dispositions – which serve us well in familiar situations will let us down when we find ourselves in a new context, either a sudden hotspot or a new level of work. The quality of thinking which was adequate for familiar situations or lower-level work is not up to meeting the demands of hotspots or higher-order work, characterized as they are by greater complexity, unpredictability, ambiguity, uncertainty, the sort of work that we start to encounter long before we get to the top (and even if we never aspire to go that far) because there can also be plenty of complexity and ambiguity *en route.*

So, to assess whether your own thinking is up to the challenge of progressing higher, look first for evidence of default thinking. It's a fair and relevant check because you were asked to reflect on a complex project or objective.

Review your notes. (Another opportunity to check out your thinking dispositions: you can also reflect on whether and how you have thought about the exercises in this chapter so far!)

Specifically,

- Has your thinking been hasty?

- Did you skip one or both of the check exercises?

- How much time did you give to these two exercises?

- Has your thinking been narrow?

- Did you think around the prompting questions?

- Did you think beyond them and come up with other questions of your own?

- Has your thinking been disorganized?

- Did you write out some notes, as suggested?

- How did you arrange those notes?

- Did you rearrange them as your thoughts became clearer?

- Has your thinking been fuzzy?

- Have you written anything down?

- If I asked you to describe your thinking now, what words would you use? Can you articulate an answer clearly and precisely?

You may well find that you are more prone to certain aspects of default thinking than others. That's a useful insight to carry forward.

Let's assume you've been prone to some default thinking. We all are. The important thing is to recognize when we're doing so and – if the situation is one that calls for it – to be able to step our thinking up a gear. It is time to turn our minds to the higher gears and to understand in more detail the dispositions that make for higher-order thinking.

Characteristics of higher-order thinking

What are the characteristics or dispositions of higher-order thinking?

- It is broad.

- It is inquisitive.

- It is deep.

- It is critical.

- It is clear.

- It is strategic.

- It is alert.

So much for the short-hand. What do these labels actually mean? What do these characteristics look like in practice?

Broad thinking is flexible, open-minded and adventurous. Broad thinkers play with ideas, explore their boundaries. They make connections which others may find unexpected or surprising. They do not permit their thinking to become limited, confined or narrow.

Inquisitive thinking is curious and inquiring. Inquisitive thinkers wonder and pose questions. They do not settle for things at face value. They show sustained rather than passing curiosity. They take time to think about different ways of defining a problem (or opportunity) before plunging into action, and remain inquisitive even then.

Critical thinking is knowledgeable, evaluative and careful. Critical thinkers insist on sound logic, relevance and rigorous argument. They differentiate evidence from mere opinion and hearsay. They call for quality evidence and corroboration and they highlight flaws in reasoning.

Deep thinking is concerned with developing reliable explanations, understanding that can be used. Deep thinkers are not satisfied with superficial reasoning that does not satisfactorily explain things. They want to understand cause and effect, the principles governing how things fit together, how they function and interact as systems over time.

Clear thinking is lucid, coherent and well-organized. Clear thinkers express thoughts in a way that is readily intelligible by others. They often ask clarifying questions or suggest alternative words or phrases to make things clearer. They are concise and precise.

Strategic thinking is forward-looking and purposeful. Strategic thinkers look ahead and think in terms of targets and objectives. They make plans and use organizers to get from now to then and from here to there. They continue to shift their attention between the future and the present, what might be and what is, between possibility and reality.

Alert thinking is the guidance system, the disposition to monitor and steer your thinking. Alert thinkers are aware of the qualities of their own and others' thinking. They monitor it, call attention to poor or inadequate thinking, and steer it in more productive directions. They are sensitive to situations that require higher-order thinking and recognize when a particular type of thinking is needed.

That's one way of describing the higher-order thinking dispositions. Very rational. Very left brain. But not so easy to commit to memory. We need to make the dispositions easier to learn, easier to remember, easier to put into practice. So here's another way of recalling the seven thinking dispositions. Much more right brain. Turn them into cartoon characters, the thinking person's equivalent of the seven dwarves, or seven film characters. Or name them after adventure characters of your choice, like the Fellowship of the Ring, or the Magnificent Seven or its Japanese samurai precursor, if you prefer. Picture them in your mind. You choose. Read the descriptions again and see what you can devise.

This is not to trivialize higher-order thinking dispositions. On the contrary, it is because the concept is so important that we need to make it stickier, mind-sized so that we can retain the core idea and recollect the rest from that, when we need it. Broad thinking in the interests of clear and strategic thinking.

Here are mine, by the way.

- The Explorer (broad thinking)

- The Detective (inquisitive thinking)

- Mr Logical (critical thinking)

- The Professor (deep thinking)

- The Newsreader (clear thinking)

- The General (strategic thinking)

- The Look-out (alert thinking).

Initially it may be a little difficult to distinguish the seven dispositions. That is natural because they are related. They are the family business, which is to do with the improvement of thinking. All in the same boat. So here's a final metaphor. Think of them as compass points, pointing out the direction in which you may need to steer your thinking next.

Alertness takes priority, literally as well as graphically, because it is the key to spotting the need, the occasion, the hotspot when it is important to use one or more of the other higher-order thinking dispositions.

So, I suggest you go back through your notes again. (Thinking about thinking needs practice.) Look for indications of the higher-order thinking dispositions. You'll probably find some. But you may not find as many as you would like. You may also find that you exhibit some more strongly than others. That's fine too. It'll highlight what you need to develop because the great news is that higher-order thinking dispositions can be developed.

Developing higher-order thinking

Here are some practical suggestions, simply expressed.

How can you make your thinking broader?

- Seek out new ideas.
- Ask for alternative points of view.
- Draw parallels and metaphors.
- Look for unusual angles.

How can you make your thinking more inquisitive?

- Look below and beyond the obvious.
- Investigate.
- Keep probing.
- Be explicitly speculative.

How can you make your thinking more critical?

- Seek out and consider substantial numbers of both pros and cons.
- Test for accuracy, relevance and thoroughness.
- Check the source of evidence.
- Examine chains of reasoning closely for gaps or convenient assumptions.

How can you make your thinking deeper?

- Look for multiple rather than single causes.

- Look for consequences and further repercussions beyond that.

- Make assessments of probability.

- Work out a model to account for patterns and interactions.

How can you make your thinking clearer?

- Collect and organize your thoughts.

- Talk to yourself. You'll quickly recognize if your thinking is lucid.

- Rehearse how you are going to express your thinking on an issue.

- Use words carefully to draw distinctions.

How can you make your thinking more strategic?

- Define your purpose. Think beyond what you want to achieve; also clarify why.

- Map out the process or sequence of moves to get from where you are to where you want to be.

- Spell out the prospective benefits of your strategy.

- Spell out and weigh up the associated costs – in various terms, including time required – for each stage of that strategy.

How can you make your thinking more alert?

- Listen for default – hasty, narrow, fuzzy and disorganized – thinking, both your own and others'.

- Know the higher-order thinking dispositions intimately.

- Watch for hotspots, contextual, mental and interactional.

- Use the language of higher-order thinking – broad, inquisitive, deep, critical, clear, strategic, alert – in your self-talk to steer your thinking.

Again, don't settle for a merely intellectual grasp of these points. That's not higher-order thinking. Go into them broadly and deeply. Be inquisitive and critical. Clarify them. Be alert and strategic. Put them to work for you. Think about your thinking.

Here are three ideas to help.

- Think carefully about your own thinking challenges. Use structured reflection to think the most demanding bits through in advance. Select and apply the tips provided to steer your thinking about the challenge in useful directions.

- Compare the people who seem to handle complex tasks easily with those who struggle. Again listen to how they talk about their work. Compare their thinking dispositions.

- Observe people in jobs bigger than your own, perhaps roles to which you aspire. Listen to how they think. You'll be surprised how much insight you can get into someone's manner of thinking, and your own, once you know what you're listening for.

Thinking hotspots

You'll have gathered from this chapter that the prime responsibility for recognizing a higher-order thinking challenge is yours. This is partly because many thinking challenges are internal – they arise when the level of the thinking that you are applying is not up to the level of the work that you are trying to do. But even when the challenges are external – in the nature of the work or situation in which you find yourself – it's still up to you to spot them.

So here are three workplace situations in which to be particularly alert. They very commonly turn out to be thinking hotspots.

First, decision-making in conditions of uncertainty. Many working situations fall into this category, such as problem-solving, investment decisions, setting objectives, committing to a proposal, or entering a joint venture. Having to make decisions under some degree of uncertainty is part of the fabric of middle- and higher-level work. It's risky. It's an occasion for higher-order thinking.

Secondly, potential conflicts and disagreements. Almost any human interaction carries the potential to fall into this category, and working interactions perhaps realize that potential more often than most. The allocation of scarce resources, competing priorities, differences of opinion and interpretation, giving feedback, offering criticism, constructive or otherwise, just going about your job in the way you think is right. All of these and more are situations that can turn into conflicts and disagreements. Again, these are high-stakes situations, both for the successful performance of work and for the effective maintenance of working relationships. They are occasions for higher-order thinking.

Thirdly, proposing and advocating. Once more it is an everyday category. These are the moments when you are putting forward a suggestion, voicing an opinion, selling a proposal, coming up with an idea, arguing for a course of action. Part of what makes this a hotspot is that these situations can so easily morph into one of the previous two categories, decision-making in conditions of uncertainty or potential conflicts and disagreements. But the particular feature of this category is that it is self-initiated. That should make it the easiest to spot. But it also makes it the thinking hotspot with the highest personal stakes. Committing yourself, exposing the quality of your thinking, putting your reputation on the line. These are situations that can make or break careers. They are certainly occasions for higher-order thinking.

Where next?

You need to be an agile thinker. But you need to bring your thinking to bear on how you work with people as well as on more docile problems. Higher-order thinking is essential, but not sufficient, for accelerating your career progression. That's where we're going next, to look at the challenges of interaction and some interactive hotspots.

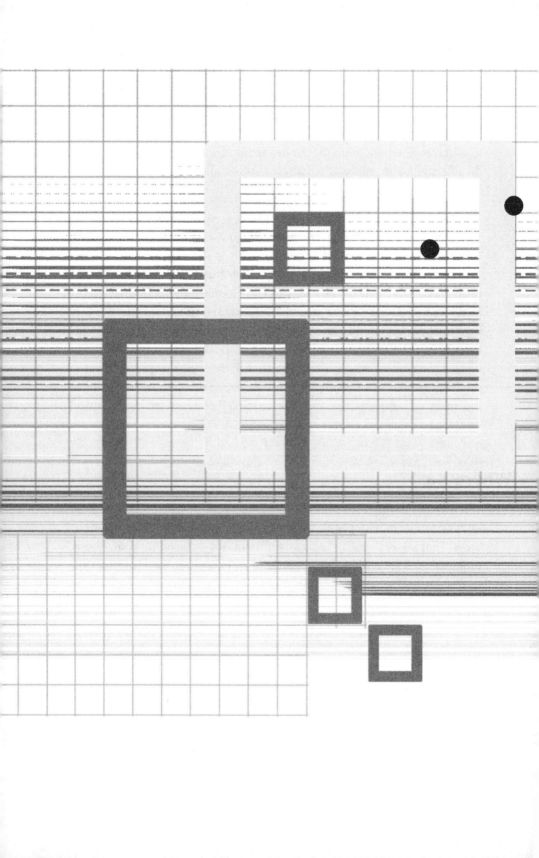

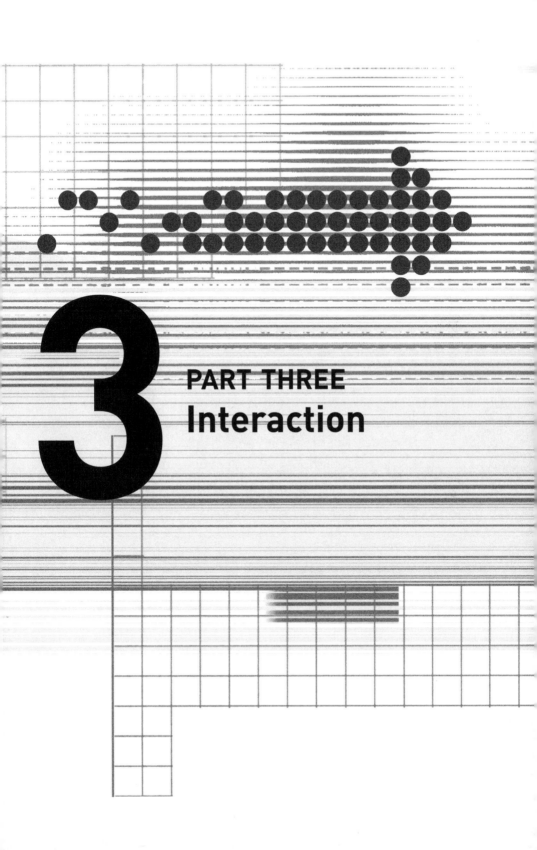

3

4 CHAPTER FOUR

Defining Moments

You are discovered, by your boss's boss, hunched over the photocopier creating a picture of your face. You have a heated disagreement with your boss, which culminates in your telling him how he should really be directing his department. You resign to enable your partner to take advantage of a career opportunity. What do you suppose these episodes do for your career?

Careers are punctuated by sudden events, like these and others quite unlike them, which can go either way. They become the real turning points in our working lives. Careers are seldom, if ever, smooth progressions from one job to the next, linked by careful appraisals of our achievements and abilities coupled with considered, objective judgements designed to match us to the next level of challenge. Real life is messier. Careers are lumpier than that. The buzz-phrase 'career progression' makes the process sound smooth. Smooth as the pages of a graduate recruitment brochure. Smooth as the wording of a recruitment advertisement. But it isn't. The grain of experience is altogether rougher. And we need to be ready for that.

You need to recognize that turning points happen. You need to recognize when you find yourself in one. Not after the event, when you have already skidded off the track and are left to pick yourself out of the wreckage.

The purpose of this chapter, then, is to alert you to defining moments.

It starts with some horror stories, as a reminder of what's at stake, to illustrate how abruptly a defining moment can occur and, above all, in the interest of higher-order thinking, to make you more alert. There is so much on our minds at work these days, so many issues clamouring for our attention, that it is easy, while getting on with the job, to lose sight of the career, to fail to recognize a defining moment.

We will also look at how to recognize defining moments at different stages in your career. Like the nature of work itself, defining moments become qualitatively different at different levels of work. And progressively harder to recognize.

Career limiting moments

If you enjoy dark humour, here's an inexhaustible source. Ask your colleagues to recall examples of 'career limiting moments' they have witnessed. Organizational life is full of them. For instance …

I had a colleague who went to collect his Chairman from the airport. He waited with the car at the appointed time and the arranged meeting point, but when there was still no sign of the Chairman, he got out, locked the car and went to look for him. He went through the terminal as quickly as he could. It was only when he got back to find the Chairman drumming his fingers impatiently on the car roof that, as he realized later, he had arrived at his career limiting moment.

Sounds ridiculous, doesn't it? Absurd that a small mishap should be so consequential for a career. But that is the nature of defining moments. They lurk in the seemingly mundane. That's how they can catch you unawares. Career limiting moments are not confined to the incompetent. If they were simply the result of incompetence, that would be fair enough. But they're not. Here's an example that a very competent colleague tells about an earlier phase of his career. Needless to say, he is not with that particular company any more.

My problem was that I had two career limiting moments in quick succession and they both occurred in the first two weeks after joining the company. My first faux pas occurred one day when my boss's boss came into the office during the morning and found us all laughing about something. He didn't say anything, just turned and went out. At lunchtime he came back and we happened to be laughing again. Again he went away without saying anything. Then about 4 o'clock in the afternoon he came in for the third time and we just happened to be laughing about something that time too. So he said, 'I can't understand it. Every time I come in here you all seem to be laughing.' I opened my mouth to say something reassuring and what I meant to say was, 'It's all right, it's not about you' but the words that actually came out were 'It's strange, isn't it, have you noticed it only happens when you come in?' Which didn't quite convey what I had intended. I could feel everybody squirming.

About three days later he caught me photocopying my head. One of my people had done a really good piece of work for me and I wanted to think of a special way of saying thank you. So I decided to make a photocopy of me smiling with 'Thank you' written on a speech bubble. Trouble was I'd had to pull my jacket up over my head to stop the light getting in and spoiling the image, so I hadn't heard him coming. Again he didn't say anything. I think he'd had his sense of humour surgically removed. Anyway, I didn't give him a chance this time. I just said, 'Ah, that's better' and walked out clutching my photocopy. But thereafter these episodes just followed me around. I know he went to my manager and said that he didn't think I should have been employed in the first place.

Two career limiting moments. The first where some words were not chosen with as much care as they might have been. A bit clumsy. A bit inattentive. And that could never be said about any of the rest of us, could it? Eh? The second where an attempt to be imaginative ended up, partly because of the first episode, looking eccentric. Yet are we not told that organizations want people to be innovative? Yes, they do. But ...

The 'but' of course has to do with other people. How other people react to what we do, or say, don't do, or don't say. Career limiting moments always occur in interaction. They are not just about us personally. That is how we can have career limiting moments – but not too many of them – in one place and yet still go on to have a successful career, but probably by moving to another place.

Career limiting moments always lurk in interactions. Remember that. Be on your guard. Here's a third example to encourage vigilance.

It was when I was working in Sales, reporting directly to the head of the European operation. I got a phone call from the President of the Company, inviting me to dinner next time he was over in London. He rang me personally from the US and arranged it.

The company's performance had been plateaued for some time, because its principal product was about twenty years old and had become dated. So over dinner I said that I thought we needed to invest in bringing our product up to date and I wasn't very flattering about my own boss in this connection.

A few months later the President fired my boss and he appointed someone else from outside, and that's when I realized that he had been interviewing me over dinner. And I'd obviously said the wrong thing as far as he was concerned. I guess he didn't like the way I'd expressed myself, because the guy he appointed was a real sleaze-ball who just kept telling the President that the product was fantastic and he loved it and could sell zillions of it. Which of course he couldn't. And didn't. But by then the damage was done, for the business and for my career there.

Career limiting moments can occur when you least expect them.

I was offered a promotion to a big staff role at HQ. I turned it down, explaining that what I really wanted next was a bigger line role in one of our operating companies. But I was pleased that I'd been approached. It seemed to mean that I was on track. The trouble was I was never asked again. I was told later that I'd been branded 'reluctant to relocate'.

But you won't always be told. Just left guessing. So be alert.

Successful moments

It's time to tell some success stories. Time to illustrate the alternative outcome. Because defining moments are not pre-determined. They are episodes which could go either way. The outcome is decided in the moment, through a combination of what you do and how that is judged by significant others.

Here's a case from the armed services, recounted by someone who went on to win the sash of honour at her officer training unit as the cadet who showed the strongest leadership qualities. The mark of a fast-tracker.

I guess the defining moment that got me the sash of honour was winning the big night exercise. There were about fifty people, divided into three competing teams, and I was in charge of one of those teams. We had to collect parts of a fire cart from dispersed grid references, assemble them and then race for home. It took all night. I think I was pretty systematic about it. I checked the particular skills and abilities of the people in my team and assigned responsibilities accordingly. And I gave some thought to the sequence of collecting the parts. You don't want to collect the axle, the heaviest bit, first and be lugging it all the way round, slowing you down and wearing you out. Having thought it through like that, the exercise was pretty straightforward, despite the darkness. Actually, the judges obviously decided that I was doing too well, because about two o'clock in the morning they suddenly gave me something else to have to think about. They announced that I now had a 'casualty' to contend with. My map-reader had officially broken both legs and could take no further active part. Anyway, I just added that to the things that had to be attended to, along with keeping everybody feeling positive and active, even though they were cold and wet and tired. And about 6am we rattled past the finish line with our 'casualty' strapped to the fire cart. The assessors must have been satisfied, because I didn't have any other major exercises to do after that.

A feature of this episode, of course, is that it was explicitly a talent-spotting exercise. It is easier, when you have been cued like that, when you know you are under the microscope, to focus your thinking, pay particular attention to what you are doing and raise your game. But defining moments are not always so clearly labelled or so easy to find. Sometimes they arise by accident.

The big defining moment in my career was when I moved from being a small fish in a big pond to being quite a big fish in a much smaller pond. I don't know that I would have thought about taking my career in that direction. It all came about because my wife got a new, bigger job in the North East. It would mean relocating, but it was a big opportunity, and we decided that she ought to take it. So I went and asked my employers if there was a job that I could get with their group somewhere in the North East. That raised my visibility. And it demonstrated that I was flexible, which was a big plus point if you wanted a career, at least it was in that organization. After that the company kept coming back to me and saying, 'We'd like you to do this next. How about it?' I didn't have to go looking for opportunities.

You might say, from this example, that defining moments are a question of mindset. Opportunities will arise, if you go looking for them. But there was no guarantee that a request for a transfer would turn out as it did. It might as easily have been the end of that individual's career in that organization. Once again, the defining nature of this episode was not immediately apparent at the time. It only became evident afterwards. Once again it was a combination of the way the individual conducted themselves in the moment, and the way that was received by others, that made the episode pivotal.

To illustrate the fleeting nature of the defining moments on which careers can turn, here is a final episode that turned out well, but could easily have worked out very differently.

The biggest turning point in my career was when I moved from a site role to a headquarters job, from being a Human Resource Director who was a generalist to become one who was an Organizational Development specialist. It all came out of a row that I had with my functional boss. To cut a long story short, there were some changes that my Managing Director and I wanted to introduce on our site, but we needed approval from the Group HR Director at HQ. Anyway, I took the proposal to him and he was going through it in great detail, questioning every aspect and anticipating all sorts of difficulties. Perhaps he was doing exactly what he needed to be doing. But at the time it just frustrated me. This was partly because I felt this was Head Office interference in what was essentially a local operational matter. But I reckon it was also because I was frustrated that my own career had got stuck in a bit of a loop, dealing with the same sort of issues all the time. Anyway, it got to a point where I closed my folder, pushed my chair back and told him that policing my proposal was not what he should be doing. He should be concentrating on being creative, on introducing longer-term organization developments and processes that would enable the business to get into shape for the demands it would face in the future. Rather tersely, he told me to leave the original proposal with him. So I got up and left the office. It was a tense parting, to say the least.

Anyway the next day he rang and said he'd been speaking with the Group Managing Director about what I'd said, and could I come along to 'complete that discussion'. I thought that might well be code for 'You're about to be sacked', so I said goodbye to my secretary and went to see him. But when I went in, he said he'd found what I'd been saying interesting and asked if I would like to be head of organization development for the Group, which hadn't consciously been in my mind at all. I'd just been letting off steam. So I was delighted and said yes. The most rewarding and fulfilling part of my career all flows from that incident.

Not all defining moments are dramatic. They can be simple, lurking in the everyday, essentially accidental.

I applied for any old job with a large company, just because I was so desperate to get out of the job I was in (I hated it so much). The company interviewed me and said I wasn't really right for the job I had applied for, but they were thinking about creating another role which would be perfect for me. They did, and it turned out to be my absolute dream job – and they gave it to me without interviewing anybody else. All because I'd originally applied for a really dull job I didn't even want.

The nature of defining moments

Enough by way of illustration. Time to summarize. What are defining moments and why do they matter?

Defining moments are …

- Turning points in career terms.

- Episodes which are disproportionately significant for our careers.

- Knife-edges: you might fall either way.

- Often disguised in seemingly innocent everyday tasks.

- Interactions with people who can influence our career prospects.

- Often sudden, unexpected and unplanned.

- Momentary or brief rather than prolonged.

- Not always easy to see in advance.

- Potentially risky if you don't appreciate what is going on.

- Critical tests of the quality of your thinking and interacting.

Defining moments are not the only important part of a career. Developing your skill sets, doing the job, producing good work, committing time and energy to the multitude of activities that are required to achieve results … all of these are necessary ingredients in career progress. Necessary but seldom sufficient. Important but not pivotal. Visibility and credibility are pivotal, and they hinge on episodes, on what occurs in the defining moments.

You have to be on the lookout for defining moments. Everyone expects to have to develop their skills to promote their career. Everyone expects to have to deliver results. Everyone expects to have to do good work to be noticed. Most people pay attention to these aspects of managing their careers. Most people neglect to pay attention to the defining moments.

Research at Harvard has suggested that 80% of the failure in human performance arises not because the individuals lack the ability to do the task in hand, nor because they lack the motivation to do it, but because they failed to recognize an occasion as one that required them to use the abilities and motivations that they already had. This is testimony to the significance of the defining moment.

An ability to recognize and navigate the defining moments will give you an edge in accelerating your career.

When to be most vigilant

You could be at a defining moment, whenever the quality of your thinking and interacting might be judged by someone whose opinion could affect your career prospects. In other words, on many occasions. You won't even be present at some of them, such as succession planning or talent review forums, so you need to make the best of the occasions when you are.

Here, then, are some of the more obvious moments – when to be most vigilant.

- At interview.
- In any other form of selection process.
- Whenever you are asked for an opinion.
- Whenever you express an opinion.
- When you are the voice of disagreement.
- Whenever you are tempted to present yourself as something you are not.
- When votes are being counted.
- When commitments, like expressions of support or opposition, are being made.
- When commitments, like promises to deliver, are being reviewed.
- When accountability rests with you.
- When your role has a high profile.

- In a situation of crisis or high risk.

- When conventions are being challenged.

- When you are among people more senior than yourself.

- When you are meeting customers or clients.

The purpose of a generic list of this sort is to give you pause for thought and to make you more alert. How many, and which, of these situations apply to you, either currently or in the foreseeable future? And what can you do about it?

Being ready for defining moments

Take another look at that list of the more obvious defining moments. At a broader level it falls into two categories: first, situations where you present yourself – for instance, when you express your opinion, initiate an action or take a position; and secondly, situations where you are evaluated by others – at interviews, reviews, discussions and other moments of decision. The other theme running through the list is that the stakes are high for someone, maybe you – in which case you should already be on alert – but maybe for someone else without you necessarily knowing about it. That's why you need to be vigilant.

So what can you do about potential defining moments?

Use higher-order thinking for a start.

- Think ahead.

- Look out for them: *Am I in the spotlight here? Who's judging?*

- Proceed with care.

- Express yourself thoughtfully.

More precisely:

- Always have your own job's 'headlines' in mind: current information on key performance indicators, market trends, what competitors are up to, the big plans for the future …

- Be relevant. Stick to the point.

- Clarify others' concerns.

- Frame and explain your views and actions by relating them to the big and pressing organizational and business issues.

- Be passionate about the bigger issues, detached about the smaller ones. (Show that you have perspective and that your energies are directed towards wider rather than more parochial concerns.)

- Regularly make time for thinking and for articulating that thinking, so that when you are suddenly called upon to express yourself, the quality of your thinking comes across.

- Use questions. If you don't have definitive answers, explain the questions and issues that you are addressing and the provisional answers that are emerging.

- Distinguish and signify how much weight you give to particular points of your own argument. It will make it easier for you to do the same with others' arguments. *This is only anecdotal at this stage. I can show you the research behind this.* (Being indiscriminate looks immature when difficult judgement calls have to be made.)

- Collect and organize your thoughts, if you need to. *Let me just think about that for a moment.* (Better to look unprepared but thoughtful than quick but incompetent.)

- Stay conspicuously open-minded during the exchange of data and information but also be clear about your own reasoning, so as not to appear indecisive.

- Look to take discussions forward – strategic thinking – into what can be done rather than backwards into what has happened.

- Be distinctive. Make contributions that are additive.

- Do not get personal about people. (You want to be, and to come across as, a bigger player, not as a brawler.)

- Work *with* other people and their inputs. Co-develop thinking, whenever possible.

- Use humour sparingly, if at all. (Humour is in the ear of the audience. People often resort to it in moments of tension, but it risks belittling you, the subject, the other person, or all three. Too risky. Stick with gravity.)

Three things are being tested in a defining moment. Your grasp of the situation. The quality of your thinking. The quality of your relating. That's why you'll recognize these ingredients in the tips that I have just provided. That's why the tips are clustered around these three issues. That's why these are the three elements of the fast track formula. That's why, if you want to advance your career, you need to have developed these capabilities so that they are second nature to you. So that they are readily available when the moment comes.

Of course, if you're really serious about accelerating your career, you won't be content to wait for defining moments to happen. You will want to create some for yourself. How do you do that?

Volunteer.

Volunteer for the difficult assignments. Volunteer for the critical projects. Go for the hot seats. Apply for the jobs in the firing line. Put yourself forward for roles that will stretch and test your mettle. I have seen people move their careers forward in leaps and bounds by doing this.

It's high risk, but high profile and potentially high return. And the advice is essentially the same. Prepare yourself. Develop and display the three capabilities. Grasp of situation. Quality of thinking. Quality of relating.

Don't volunteer without them.

Here are four other don'ts, if you want to avoid defining moments becoming career limiting moments.

- Don't pretend to be someone you're not. (You'll be found out in the end, if not sooner.)

- Don't wing it, or make it up as you go along, when you are put on the spot. (Better to show that you know what you need to find out than that you don't know what you're talking about.)

- Don't court favour. (It compromises both your integrity and your value, by undermining your ability to make a distinctive personal contribution.)

- Don't expect what worked in your previous job to work in your next one. (Even small shifts in context have significant implications for the patterns of relating that are involved and the thinking that is required.)

So don't imagine you can relax as your career progresses. You need to become even more alert. Here's why …

Progressively harder to spot

Defining moments become harder to spot as your career progresses. In the earlier stages of a career the rules of the game are generally made reasonably clear and this gives you an easier opportunity to rise to the expectation. During this phase, when the career mills are still at the early stages of their sorting processes and want plenty of raw material to choose from, the defining moments are usually well sign-posted. The selection interview with specified criteria. The particular course or qualification that is known to be a pre-requisite for entry. The assessment or development centres – 'screening camps' – which are used to find the pick of the crop and to tell people how far they match up. The performance appraisal, where the feedback is spelled out. For instance …

I was yellow-carded. 'I have been reviewing your performance appraisal … you will no doubt appreciate that it will be impossible for us to consider you for more senior appointments in the future, unless … '. I replied formally. 'Please forgive my delay in replying … ' My letter was deemed 'a most constructive and positive response'. Shortly after that I was promoted to Marketing Director.

Later, however, the 'rules of the game' change, as another interviewee recalled …

I had a fellow Director who had an unfortunate habit of falling asleep in meetings. After the fourth time the MD said, 'Enough's enough' so we had to find 'a different solution'.

Note two particular features of this little anecdote. Fourth offence before the red card. Would that be likely in a lower- or even a middle-level role? More interestingly, notice the phrase, 'find a different solution'. Very delicate, very refined. Nothing so vulgar as a good bollocking. A real insight into the culture of this particular senior management community.

It is not just that the goalposts move. They also become less explicit.

This is why search consultants – head-hunters – spend so long screening candidates for senior positions, and why most of that time is given over to assessing for 'fit' or 'the chemistry'. This is why high-flying cadets are assigned as Personal Assistants to Senior Officers and up-and-coming managers as Executive Assistants to Chief Executives. In these work-shadowing roles they can be inducted into and absorb the unspoken rules of conduct from an established role model in the domain.

As one interviewee put it,

I'd moved around a lot and I thought I was good at recognizing and adapting to different types of organization. But what I hadn't taken into account was how much the culture of the senior management setting could vary from one organization to another. The implicit rules of the game in the old context simply did not apply in the new one.

Or as another put it, even more succinctly,

You have to do a lot of decoding when you get into the upper echelons. I wasn't interested in being promoted any further, because I just wasn't prepared to play the game.

The paradox of progression

There is a massive paradox at the heart of career progression. Becoming more senior entails becoming more, rather than less, dependent on other people. You would expect that career advancement would make you more powerful and less dependent, and in some respects – principally economic – it does, but in the practical sense of getting work done, progressing renders you more dependent on others. As you move further from the front-line of the action, your own contribution becomes increasingly indirect. You become more dependent on others to translate your ideas and directions into action, more dependent on others to provide you with accurate information and feedback, more dependent on the quality of your relationships to get things done. Your continuing success becomes increasingly dependent on your ability to relate. Consequently, and for most people unexpectedly, interpersonal skills become more rather than less important as their careers progress.

Before turning in the next chapter to how you can develop influential relating skills, let's look at what you should definitely *not* bring to the party ...

Fatal incompetencies: reasons you might not get promoted

Various researchers have looked at the sort of characteristics that can cause a career to 'derail', because of their adverse impact on relationships. When detachment becomes aloofness, for instance, or charm becomes manipulation. Particularly important in this field are those characteristics whose impact is relatively inconsequential in lower-level work, but which become increasingly significant in higher-level roles, to the point that they can fatally undermine your career progress.

You can find out more from EDAC (Executive Development Assessment Centre), an expert web-based provider of methods for assessing people's capabilities and potential [www.edacen.com]. Drawing on years of research into the competencies required by strategic leaders, EDAC looks particularly carefully for the characteristics which can impair effective performance at higher levels of work. These destructive tendencies, or 'inhibitors', include: 'technical shortcomings', selfishness, arrogance, micro-management (or interference), explosive temper and inaccessibility. The point here, of course, is that all of these characteristics are essentially failures in relating to others.

Let's briefly look at each of them more closely.

Technical shortcomings is a phrase to describe people who lack the know-how required to do their job. The real consequence of this tendency, however, is that you will fail to secure the respect or co-operation of others. This is the recurring feature of all these 'career incompetencies'.

Selfishness is how you will be labelled if you abuse your position to serve your own interests, whether by giving yourself special advantages or taking the credit for work done by others. Again, it is the effect that this characteristic has on relationships which makes it so destructive. It alienates people.

So does arrogance. If your behaviour is self-important, or you belittle people by patronizing or talking down to them, you won't secure others' commitment.

Interference has a similar effect. Micro-managing the people who work for you conveys the message that you do not trust them, and a perception of being distrusted breeds distrust in return. It creates a vicious cycle. Interestingly, the research suggests that those who interfere and micro-manage often have strong needs for control. They frequently exhibit rigid rather than higher-order patterns of thought, oversimplifying complexity and risk through unsophisticated, black-and-white thinking. They also tend to take on subordinates' work as an escape from the more complex activities in which they themselves should properly be engaged.

Explosive temper may also reflect a shortfall in thinking capabilities, an inability to grasp complex problems. It is certainly another characteristic that undermines the development of influence or respect and so subverts the quality relationships that are so vital if you are in higher-level work, given your dependence on others.

A final destructive characteristic, for those who aspire to do higher-level work, is inaccessibility. Whether this is the product of poor interpersonal skills or self-centredness, its effect is to render you out of touch. This undermines every aspect of the fast track formula. It interrupts the ability to obtain, and maintain, a realistic grasp of context. It starves higher-order thinking. It denies influential interactions.

But the failure to achieve influential relating is not simply another manifestation of lower-order thinking. Smart people can also neglect this aspect of the fast track formula, this ingredient of successful career progression. It's not sufficient to have higher-order thinking capabilities unless you can also recognize – and aim them at – the interpersonal challenges that come with your level of work. Yale Professor of Psychology, Robert Sternberg, provides extensive evidence of this in an edited collection of research papers, *Why Smart People Can Be So Stupid* [Yale University Press, 2002]. Contributing to this collection, his colleague Richard Wagner cites research identifying the following characteristics as distinguishing features of failed managers, those whose careers falter rather than fly:

- Inability to build a cohesive team.

- Over- or under-managing.

- Overly ambitious.

- Unsupportive, and demanding, of subordinates.

- Overly emotional.

- Insensitive, cold and arrogant.

- Poor relationships with staff.

- Overriding personality defects.

It is a list remarkably similar to EDAC's 'inhibitors'. And again, the unifying theme is the individual's failure to achieve influential relating. Beware of these tendencies. Work to remedy them now, unless you want your career to fall victim to them later.

Interaction hotspots

These are, in theory, the easiest to recognize, because they generally involve other people. But here are three types of interaction to which you should pay particular attention. They are less obvious, but may be no less hot.

First, peer group interactions. Bosses and customers are obvious stakeholders. You are likely to keep your wits about you in your dealings with them, although familiarity often causes people to let their attention lapse even here. Peer relationships, however, are more often a blind spot. Neglect the quality of your relating here at your peril, because patterns of peer relationships change. For all sorts of reasons other people may get promoted before you do. Cultivating trust in your peer relationships will produce allies or at least neutrals above you, not enemies.

Secondly, invisible relationships. Not all relationships are immediately apparent. Nor is relating simply a series of bilateral connections. Joining a new department, team, project or organization will take you into a new web of relationships. It takes time to discover the networks and connections, who talks to whom and who listens to whom. Invest some of your energy in finding your way around this informal dimension of your organization. Until you do, take particular care about what you say, especially when asked for your opinion about others.

Thirdly, interactions at the edge of your comfort zone. This category concerns another form of relating, how you relate with situations that you don't enjoy or find more testing. Pay particular attention to these, because they point to the edge of your confidence and competence. If you want to give yourself an edge, then you'll focus your development on the issues that you find here, although you may find you need the help of a coach to get inside the problem and figure out a way forward. The clues for this sort of hotspot are in your own feelings and behaviours, often in a sense of anxiety about a forthcoming task and in procrastination, delay or some other form of avoidance. You're unlikely to be able to accelerate your career unless you deal with defining moments of this sort.

Where next?

We've seen that careers can turn on defining moments, a particular type of hotspot, which have disproportionate impact. We've also established that what makes a defining moment is the way in which the quality of either or both of your thinking and your relating are judged by a significant other. We've looked previously at how to develop higher-order thinking. It's time to turn to how you can develop your capability in terms of higher-order, influential relating. It is the final element in the fast track formula.

5

CHAPTER FIVE

Influential Relating

Relating is vital for career progress. The people who command attention, who win others' support, co-operation, endorsement and approval, who gain others' trust and access to opportunities, are the people who relate well.

There is a growing appreciation of the importance of relating well. It is reflected in the contemporary interest in modelling exceptional performance through NLP (neuro-linguistic programming) and in the not unrelated subject of Emotional Intelligence, popularized by American psychologist Daniel Goleman.

Yet it will always be easy to relate badly, especially in our occupational lives. It will be easy because our first preoccupation is usually with the job in hand, on the task that we are trying to complete, rather than on the other people involved in the process. But we are always relating. Every interaction is a form of relating. And every pattern of interaction carries potential consequences for the quality of the subsequent relationship. Every interaction is potentially a defining moment. So, relating well – becoming influential in your relationships – is a function of how you shape your interactions.

This chapter is about making your interactions influential.

It is also long. That's because it needs to cover the variety of ways in which people can interact. Inevitably, some of these are going to be more relevant and interesting to you than others. So feel free to concentrate on those and treat the rest as a source of reference, unless or until any of them become useful for you personally. To help you to decide which bits are most immediately important, let's start by forming some idea of how you currently prefer to relate.

Five ways of relating

A particularly useful model of human interaction (the *Conflict–Mode Instrument*) was created by organizational consultants Ken Thomas and Ralph Kilmann to explore the different ways in which interpersonal conflicts can be handled [Consulting Psychologists Press, 1974]. They identified five distinct approaches:

- Competing.

- Avoiding.

- Accommodating.

- Collaborating.

- Compromising.

Typically, individuals prefer certain approaches, making more use of those and less of the others. As you read the following short definitions, identify the one or two approaches which you tend to use most.

Competing is a forceful, and forcing, approach, which seeks to dominate the interaction.

Avoiding is a style which seeks to avert disagreement either by staying away from particular issues altogether or by approaching them in an indirect, diplomatic or tactful way.

Accommodating is an unassertive, concessionary approach that tends to give way, or simply give in, often with a view to preserving, or trying to develop, a relationship with the other person.

Collaborating is a co-operative style, which is also assertive, seeking to resolve the subject matter of the interaction through developing a shared understanding and robust discussion of the issues involved.

Compromising is an approach that is prepared to give and take in the interest of fairness or of finding common ground without undue delay or confrontation.

You might find it useful to note *your* dominant styles on this diagram, like
this ●

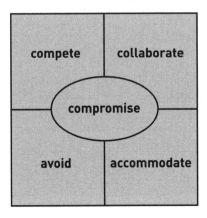

These five approaches are essentially the choices that you face in a situation
of conflict or *prospective* conflict. The fact that people can, and do, adopt an
approach *in anticipation* of a possible disagreement is what makes the
model particularly potent. It is more than a description of how people
behave once a disagreement has erupted. It is a description of how people
tend to go about any interaction in which there is potential for conflict or
disagreement. And that is virtually any human interaction. The model is
therefore a way of looking at patterns of human interaction in general.

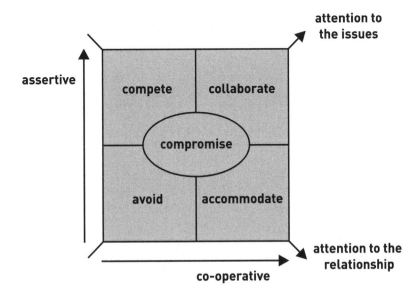

These various approaches, and the underlying differences among them – in terms of lower and higher assertiveness, co-operation, attention to relationship and attention to issues – can be usefully mapped as shown.

The limitation of the original model, however, is that it focuses specifically on the individual. This makes its depiction of human interactions not only one-sided but also artificially static. Disagreements, like other interactions, are dynamic. Each of the people involved may shift from one style to another during the course of the interaction, and at any point in time the two are often in different styles. That is one reason why conflicts can become prolonged.

To help you quickly get value from what follows, you might also find it useful at this stage to think about someone with whom you have to work. What approaches do they tend to use? Mark them like this ◯

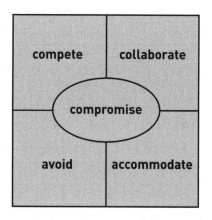

What follows is my development from the Thomas–Kilmann starting point to turn the framework into a more dynamic way of looking at patterns of relating. This makes it more useful for understanding the range and implications of the choices open to you in how you conduct your dealings with other people. And for understanding how you are perceived by those people. Managing those perceptions is immensely important, especially in the defining moments of your career and as your success becomes increasingly dependent on the quality of your relating with others.

To keep it manageable, we are going to look at patterns of one-to-one interaction. That will be complex enough. With five approaches open to each party, that gives twenty-five possible patterns of interaction. Add more people and the proceedings obviously become exponentially more complex. This, of course, is one reason why group meetings can become such difficult contexts in which to achieve productive work. However, for our purpose, the range of one-to-one possibilities should be sufficient to illustrate and explain the dynamics of influential – and uninfluential – patterns of relating.

Here is the format for what follows. First, the pattern of relating is placed into a simplified version of the interactions map. Your approach is indicated by the black dot, theirs by the white dot.

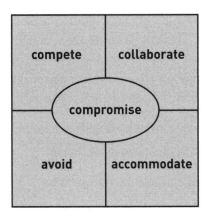

Conceptual maps of this sort can be helpful for clarifying complex situations, and also for transferring ideas into practice across a variety of situations. The map shows how each of you is approaching the interaction. Then the pattern of interaction is described in several ways, because, of course, how it is seen and experienced depends on the perspective of the individual concerned. So, each pattern is described in the first, second and third person; as it might be perceived by you, by the other person involved and by an objective bystander, respectively. This third perspective is reinforced by also suggesting a name for each pattern, as it might appear to the outsider. This is to encourage you to take a more detached perspective. You need to apply higher-order thinking to your relating, just as you need to apply it to your other mental challenges.

Each pattern is assessed in terms of its potential for influential relating. Then the interaction is described from a fourth perspective, as a coach offering advice. This fourth voice offers tips, and some words of caution, for improving that interaction, for turning it into more productive and influential relating. Because relating is a dynamic process, the final offering is a return to the map, pointing out an additional move that might be smart when you find yourself in this pattern.

In each case the darker figure represents you, the first person. Imagine yourself in that position.

Assume that you have the prime responsibility for shaping the pattern of the interaction. It's a good assumption to make, if you want to shape the progress of your career.

This is a big chapter. There is a lot here. You aren't expected to take it all in, rather to get the gist and to get into the habit of attending to patterns of relating. Consult these maps for reference until the idea becomes sufficiently familiar. The patterns are clustered in groups of five, revolving around the particular strategy adopted by the first person, by you. I have labelled these strategies:

- Competitive (forcing approaches).

- Avoiding (reluctant approaches).

- Accommodating (befriending approaches).

- Collaborative (joint problem-solving approaches).

- Compromising (give and take approaches).

Recall which of the five approaches you tend to use most often. I suggest taking that, or those, as your starting point. There is a direction-finder below that will guide you to the relevant page.

Alternatively, you may wish to read right through to get a feel for each of the five strategies. Or you may prefer to focus on a few patterns of relating that seem familiar. Pay particular attention to patterns that resonate with your own experience. Whichever way you go about it, take some time. Avoid defaulting into haste. Higher-order thinking will produce more benefit.

Your Approach	Their Approach	Page
Competitive	Competitive	85
Competitive	Collaborative	86
Competitive	Avoiding	87
Competitive	Accommodating	88
Competitive	Compromising	89

The competitive (forcing) postures

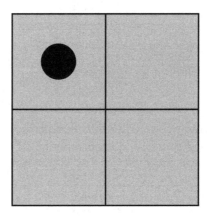

Competitive postures often reflect a strong achievement drive, a belief that the best way to get things done is by being forceful. Forcefulness works better when others are dependent on you. It tends not to work when you are more dependent on others, which – as we have seen – paradoxically tends to become increasingly the case as your career progresses.

Competitive approaches are a very risky strategy for influential relating.

They produce these patterns of relating (in no particular order):

1. The battleground.

2. The missed opportunity.

3. Cat and mouse.

4. Master and servant.

5. Hard bargaining.

1. The battleground

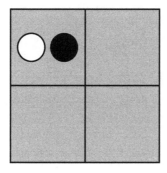

Implicit messages:

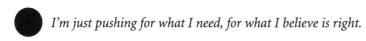

I'm just pushing for what I need, for what I believe is right.

This is what happens when you try to push me around. Come on then, if you think you're hard enough!

The detached observer's view: *This is a fight, a trial of strength. Sooner or later someone's going to get injured. The relationship is probably being damaged already.*

Potential for influential relating: LOW

Advice: This essentially confrontational pattern of relating needs to be used very selectively. As a weapon of last resort. It puts the prospect of a constructive ongoing relationship too much at risk. Before pushing so hard for a particular outcome, focus first on understanding all the issues, from both perspectives, theirs and yours; reframe the interaction to make it more like joint problem-solving.

A Smart Move from this situation ...

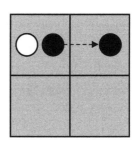

2. The missed opportunity

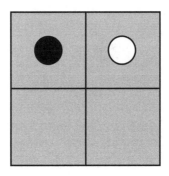

Implicit messages:

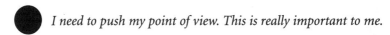

I need to push my point of view. This is really important to me.

You don't have to be so pushy; I'm willing to get to grips with the issues here, but we can't just look at one side of things.

The observer's view: *'me' vs 'us'. They could work this out, if one of them wasn't blundering around like a hippopotamus, making so much noise.*

Potential for influential relating: LOW

Advice: You may be pushing unnecessarily. You may already have got your point across. The other person is trying to understand the issues, is open to working with you to resolve them, but you run the risk of preventing that by sounding self-centred. Listen to what the other person is trying to contribute to the proceedings and consider whether that offers a way of arriving at a win:win outcome.

A Smart Move from this situation ...

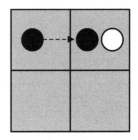

3. Cat and mouse

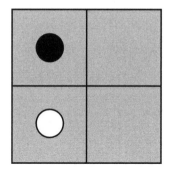

Implicit messages:

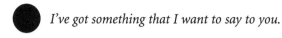

I've got something that I want to say to you.

I don't want to talk about it; certainly not at the moment.

The observer's view: *Hunter and quarry; one chasing and one running away!*

Potential for influential relating: LOW

Advice: Stop chasing. Rephrase what you want to say. Frame it in terms of an issue that is a shared concern or interest. Recognize that this may not be the most appropriate time to discuss it. Seek to fix a time when it can be discussed. Offer the prospect of some give and take, but be careful not to go too far towards making one-sided concessions.

A Smart Move from this situation …

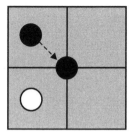

4. Master and servant

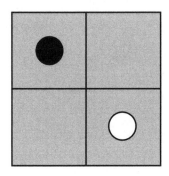

Implicit messages:

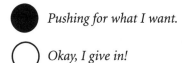

Pushing for what I want.

Okay, I give in!

The observer's view: *A case of domination. Winner and loser. The Master and the servant. I wonder if the servant will look to get their own back?*

Potential for influential relating: LOW

Advice: You're going to get what you want on this occasion, but be mindful of the damage you may be doing to the relationship. It would be smart to check how the other person is feeling. Are they making a willing concession or are you forcing it out of them? Might there be more value for the on-going relationship, if you were to demonstrate a bit more give-and-take?

A Smart Move from this situation ...

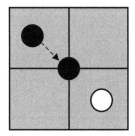

5. Hard bargaining

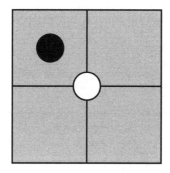

Implicit messages:

 I'm going to push you on this.

 I'm willing to compromise a bit.

The observer's view: *This could go either way. There is some willingness to be more flexible, but this isn't getting a response yet. If the common ground isn't explored, this could turn into a battleground.*

Potential for influential relating: LOW

Advice: Be careful! Does it make sense to go on being so forceful when the other person is willing to give and take? You could pay in terms of goodwill. It might be appropriate for you to be insistent, but you'd better explain your reasoning carefully, or it's likely that you'll come across as inflexible. You're more likely to relate if you reciprocate the give-and-take.

A Smart Move from this situation …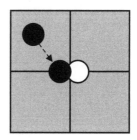

The avoiding (reluctant) postures

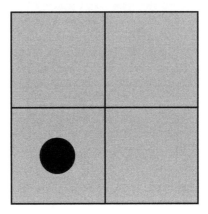

Avoiding postures are more complex. They usually reflect an anxiety, but the precise nature of this can vary. It might come from an intrinsic discomfort with conflict, or it might signify a more political stance, a watchfulness, or opportunistic way of getting things done.

Generally, avoiding postures are a risky strategy for influential relating.

They produce these patterns of relating (in no particular order):

1. Run away!

2. Differing priorities.

3. Conspiracy of silence.

4. Sulking in the corner.

5. Heel dragging.

1. Run away!

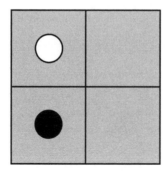

Implicit messages:

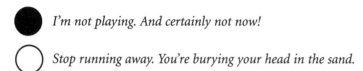

● *I'm not playing. And certainly not now!*

○ *Stop running away. You're burying your head in the sand.*

The detached observer's view: *Avoidance tactics in the extreme. One of them wants something and the other doesn't want to get involved. The problem is, we can't tell why.*

Potential for influential relating: LOW

Advice: You're probably coming across as if you're running away, or sulking. Maybe you don't care for the pushy way the other person is behaving, but avoiding them isn't going to give you a long-term solution. Focus on, and speak up about, the issues that concern you both since that offers the prospect of a more rational conversation. At the very least, indicate when you are going to be willing to discuss the matter.

A Smart Move from this situation …

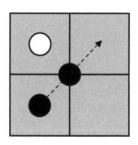

2. Differing priorities

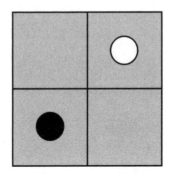

Implicit messages:

 Not now.

○ *You and I need to get to grips with this.*

The observer's view: *This looks like evasion. If the timing isn't right, or if there is some other issue, then it would be much better to explain that.*

Potential for influential relating: LOW

Advice: You're coming across as if this issue is not one of your priorities. And perhaps it isn't. But you're also coming across as if you don't have time for this person, and as if you're not prepared to work with them. There is a real danger in being perceived in these ways. Find out why the other person regards the issue as so pressing, and at least agree when you are going to be able to discuss it.

A Smart Move from this situation …

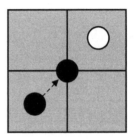

3. Conspiracy of silence

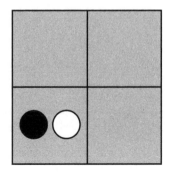

Implicit messages:

 Don't want to talk about it.

 Nor me.

The observer's view: *Looks as if they're agreeing not to talk about it. Wonder what it is? And why they're keeping so quiet about it?*

Potential for influential relating: MODERATE

Advice: There are confidences, issues that should not be discussed. But the risk in this pattern is that you are being complicit in ignoring something that deserves greater attention or priority. Take care not to default into this pattern by leaving important matters implicit or unspoken. This is an essentially closed posture and the cost you might eventually have to pay is high because trust is the price to be paid for a lack of openness. Exploring whether there are issues that need to be discussed may be a better move.

A Smart Move from this situation ...

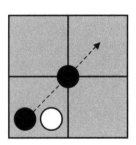

4. Sulking in the corner

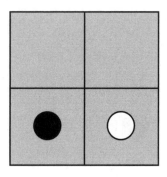

Implicit messages:

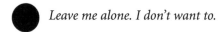 *Leave me alone. I don't want to.*

Why are you avoiding me? I want us to make friends.

The observer's view: *This person is not responding to the overture. Hmm … I wonder what they're worried about?*

Potential for influential relating: LOW

Advice: You are getting an invitation. Does it really make sense to continue to stand off? Bear in mind the investment of 'face' that the other person is already making, especially if this is to repair the relationship. Think how much more damage you might do to the relationship by refusing to acknowledge the gesture. Accepting a share of the responsibility for the pair of you getting into this position is likely to make amends and establish a stronger ongoing relationship.

A Smart Move from this situation …

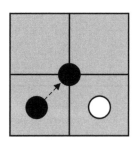

5. Heel dragging

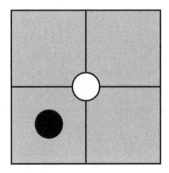

Implicit messages:

 It feels as if I'm being pushed. I'm not ready to commit.

 Come on, we can reach some sort of agreement over this.

The observer's view: *One's willing to move, but the other is reluctant.*

Potential for influential relating: LOW

Advice: In offering some sort of compromise the other person almost certainly feels that they are being fair and reasonable. By the same token, if you do not respond in the same way, they are likely to consider that you are acting unfairly and unreasonably. Not surprisingly, the effect will be to degrade the relationship and your capacity to be influential with this person in the future.

A Smart Move from this situation …

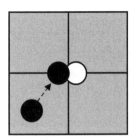

The accommodating (befriending) postures

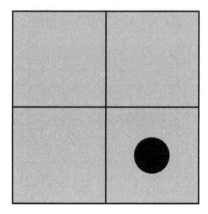

Accommodating postures are essentially befriending strategies. They may come from a desire to be liked, or from a belief that building relationships is a priority because it provides the foundation on which to get things done where others are involved.

Accommodating postures are a moderately effective strategy for influential relating.

They produce these patterns of relating (in no particular order):

1. The concession.

2. Relationship before issue.

3. Repairing the damage.

4. Collegiality.

5. Bending over backwards.

1. The concession

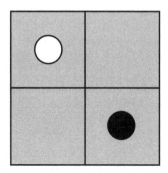

Implicit messages:

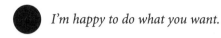 *I'm happy to do what you want.*

○ *This really matters to me. I need you to do this for me.*

The detached observer's view: *There is a favour being offered here, or a peace-making gesture. Clearly one of them considers the relationship to be important.*

Potential for influential relating: MODERATE

Advice: Concessions and favours can be powerful ways of developing a relationship, but be careful not to overdo it. That quickly serves to devalue the favour. And be sure that you do not remain in this position because you are being dominated. If that is the case, then respond with more assertion, preferably by calling attention to the issue of mutual concern that needs to be addressed, rather than simply by mirroring the other person's forcefulness.

An alternative move …

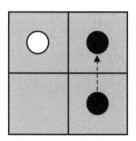

2. Relationship before issue

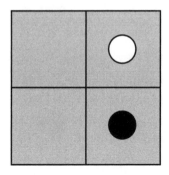

Implicit messages:

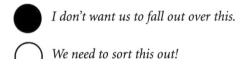

I don't want us to fall out over this.

We need to sort this out!

The observer's view: *There's a risk here that emphasizing the relationship will leave an important issue unresolved, and the relationship is ultimately weakened rather than strengthened.*

Potential for influential relating: MODERATE

Advice: A classic human dilemma: whether to give priority to the issue at hand or to the relationship with the other person. In this posture you are opting to attend to the relationship, while the other person's focus is on the issue. Given that they are looking to work together with you to sort the matter out, it is more likely to be productive, both in the shorter and the longer term, for you to join them in collaborative problem-solving than in trying to draw them, against their will, into setting it aside in the interests of friendship.

An alternative move ...

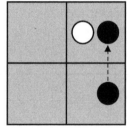

3. Repairing the damage

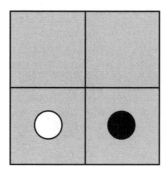

Implicit messages:

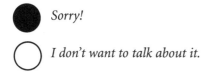

● *Sorry!*

○ *I don't want to talk about it.*

The observer's view: *The overture is not being accepted.*

Potential for influential relating: HIGH

Advice: An important pattern to have in your repertoire. At some time or another you are bound to owe someone an apology. In those circumstances, it is better made sooner rather than later. Even then, you may find the other person reluctant to respond to your gesture. Don't give up. Now is not the moment to justify yourself or to look for a rational discussion. Those approaches may simply add insult to injury. Concentrate first on repairing the relationship. It is best to say sorry. Alternatively, wait for a better moment.

An alternative move ...

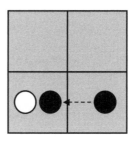

4. Collegiality

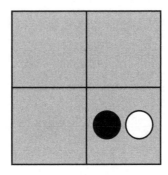

Implicit messages:

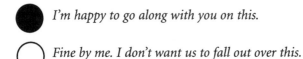

I'm happy to go along with you on this.

Fine by me. I don't want us to fall out over this.

The observer's view: *This is putting teamwork first.*

Potential for influential relating: MODERATE

Advice: Another useful pattern. There are times when establishing, maintaining or developing the relationship is the best investment you can make. By accenting your willingness to co-operate, you may earn the trust which will permit you to be more assertive when particular issues require you to be. But be careful that important issues are not neglected, for fear of upsetting teamwork.

An alternative move ...

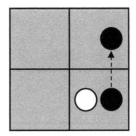

5. Bending over backwards

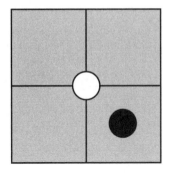

Implicit messages:

 Whatever you want! I don't want us to fall out over this.

 Would you be prepared to do one more thing?

The observer's view: *This looks like weakness.*

Potential for influential relating: LOW

Advice: A pattern to be used sparingly. Are you giving in too readily? Is the other person taking advantage of your relationship? If you feel uncomfortable on either count, then respond by being more assertive, either about what you personally need in this particular situation, or in terms of issues or concerns that the suggested concession might cause for both of you. Moving into a joint problem-solving posture will probably do more to maintain the relationship (as well as your self-respect and their respect for you) than sliding into mirroring the other person's bargaining mode.

An alternative move ...

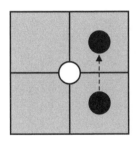

The collaborative (joint problem-solving) postures

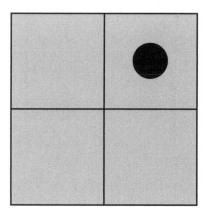

Collaborative postures are rational and systematic, essentially the thinking person's approach to getting things done with others. They can spring from a belief that developing a shared understanding is the best way to progress an issue. This produces another paradox, albeit a more pleasant one, which is that the approach with the most to offer is also the easiest to learn, since it is essentially a matter of technique.

Collaborative postures are a highly effective strategy for influential relating.

They produce these patterns of relating (in no particular order):

1. Modifying the battering ram.

2. Thoroughly win:win.

3. Raising the priority.

4. Don't just agree with me. Have we resolved it?

5. Not leaving things half-cooked.

1. Modifying the battering ram

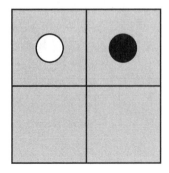

Implicit messages:

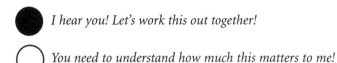 *I hear you! Let's work this out together!*

You need to understand how much this matters to me!

The observer's view: *What might have been just an argument is becoming a rigorous and productive discussion.*

Potential for influential relating: HIGH

Advice: The key point here is not to give up on your collaborative problem-solving approach, tempting as that might be when the other person is taking a more parochial or self-centred approach. You have to shape the interaction so that it takes place in your mode. That will be more productive, both in terms of resolving the issues and in terms of making your ongoing relationship more influential. This is a pattern for ensuring that assertive exchanges produce useful outcomes. Again, the variation is to be the one who *proposes* greater flexibility, if required.

An alternative move …

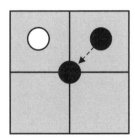

2. Thoroughly win:win

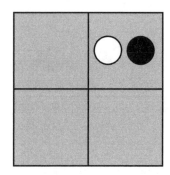

Implicit messages:

 Let's work together to really sort this out.

 I'd like to see if we can resolve this jointly.

The detached observer's view: *This shows that two heads can be better than one.*

Potential for influential relating: HIGH

Advice: Not much advice needed here. This pattern produces influential relating because it explicitly focuses on understanding and seeking to resolve all the issues involved in a situation, as perceived by both parties. It encourages both co-operation and assertiveness on the part of both. The impression that this pattern of interaction creates is rational, objective, professional. Not surprisingly it fosters trust. One word of caution: because it is necessarily time-consuming, it may be helpful to relax this approach into a more flexible, compromising style, as mutually agreed priorities dictate.

An alternative move ...

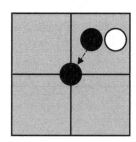

3. Raising the priority

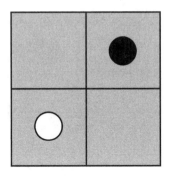

Implicit messages:

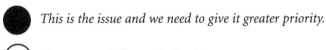

This is the issue and we need to give it greater priority.

I'm not sure if I'm ready for this.

The observer's view: *This is raising the issue; it's bold because there's some reluctance around, but it's being done in a way that encourages involvement, so that's helpful.*

Potential for influential relating: HIGH

Advice: Generally, this is an influential pattern, calling attention to important issues and encouraging involvement by engaging in a collaborative approach to tackling them. The important refinement is to be sensitive to the other person's reluctance, which is difficult if you don't understand it. But it may be difficult for them to disclose it, if they don't feel they can trust you yet. So, a move towards relating for the sake of trust may be useful.

An alternative move ...

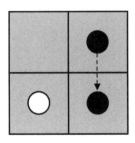

4. Don't just agree with me. Have we resolved it?

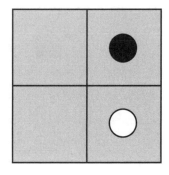

Implicit messages:

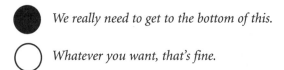 *We really need to get to the bottom of this.*

Whatever you want, that's fine.

The observer's view: *They're going along together, but it looks as if one of them is really signed up and the other one doesn't want to cause an upset.*

Potential for influential relating: MODERATE

Advice: Again, this pattern reflects the dilemma of whether to give priority to the issue at hand or to the relationship with the other person. In this case you are opting to focus on the issue, while the other person is concentrating on the relationship. Aim to make it easy for the other person to speak out about anything that is still concerning them, but that they are reluctant to say. This might entail a move indicating more flexibility on your part.

An alternative move ...

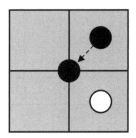

5. Not leaving things half-cooked

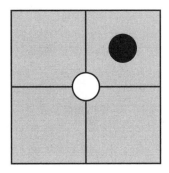

Implicit messages:

 We need to sort this matter out once and for all.

 We could find a solution that's good enough for the time being.

The observer's view: *Agreeing that they both need to do something, but disagreeing on how far to go with it.*

Potential for influential relating: HIGH

Advice: This is a pattern which commonly emerges when the two parties agree that a topic is important, but have different views about the degree of its importance or priority. Where the issue presents significant risks or repercussions, your pressing for a more rigorous resolution is appropriate and likely to strengthen your subsequent influence. Take care not to insist on this approach indiscriminately, because it is time-consuming and will make you appear inflexible.

An alternative move ...

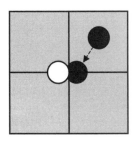

The compromising (give and take) postures

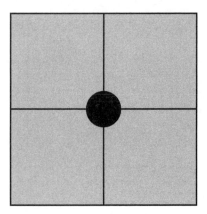

Compromising postures may spring either from a strong sense that fairness should be the basis for getting things done or simply from pragmatism, the belief that expediency is an essential ingredient in making things happen.

Compromising postures are a moderately effective strategy for influential relating.

They produce these patterns of relating (in no particular order):

1. Open for negotiation.

2. Short-cutting.

3. Coaxing.

4. Wringing it.

5. Give and take.

1. Open for negotiation

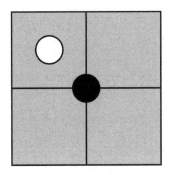

Implicit messages:

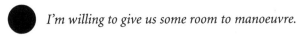 *I'm willing to give us some room to manoeuvre.*

Here's what I'm looking for.

The detached observer's view: *Flexible! If this overture doesn't get a response, there's still scope to be constructively assertive by calling for a thorough joint examination of their respective issues and concerns.*

Potential for influential relating: MODERATE

Advice: An important move to have in your repertoire. It is too easy, and dangerous, to match someone else's competing posture. The effect is generally an escalation into the contest of the battlefield. A more constructive move is to invite some give and take, perhaps by suggesting some common ground. However, be careful that you don't just start sliding! That will appear as weakness. Clarify the basis on which you would be prepared to relax your own needs in the interests of avoiding an impasse and finding some common ground.

An alternative move …

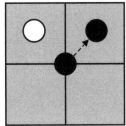

2. Short-cutting

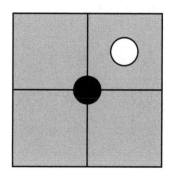

Implicit messages:

 Here's a quicker way.

 We need to sort these things out once and for all.

The observer's view: *Looks like a desire to hurry things along.*

Potential for influential relating: MODERATE

Advice: The issue at the heart of this pattern is about how much time you can give to achieving a resolution. The other person is willing to work with you, but the process feels as if it is becoming too protracted from your point of view. You are making what you consider to be flexible suggestions, and the risk is that you will become frustrated with their seemingly ponderous, or even pedantic, approach. Find out why they believe that a more rigorous approach is necessary in this situation. Ask yourself whether you might be rushing things. Might you get a more robust outcome, and a stronger on-going relationship, by seeking a more rigorous resolution? Alternatively, you may simply have to persevere with your flexible exploration of alternatives to find one that is good enough for both of you.

An alternative move ...

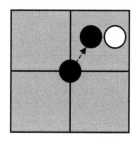

3. Coaxing

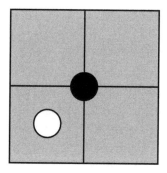

Implicit messages:

 Look, suppose we agree to do things like this.

 I don't feel ready to commit.

The observer's view: *Looks like encouraging rather than forcing. They are certainly attempting to get things moving jointly rather than unilaterally.*

Potential for influential relating: HIGH

Advice: Another important pattern to have in your set. There will be plenty of cases when the person you are dealing with is reluctant and does not feel ready to commit, even to discussing an issue, far less coming to an agreement about it. They may well have good reasons for that. Try first to reassure them by understanding their reluctance rather than pressing on too forcefully for a resolution of the issue as you see it. Coaxing them towards being more assertive about their own views and interests, and into being more willing to work jointly on the issues with you, can be a useful demonstration of flexibility and trustworthiness on your part.

An alternative move ...

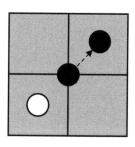

4. Wringing it

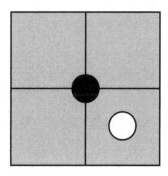

Implicit messages:

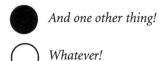

⚫ *And one other thing!*

⚪ *Whatever!*

The observer's view: *Pushy! Is this going too far?*

Potential for influential relating: LOW

Advice: Like any pattern of relating where one party is being more assertive than the other, the risk here is that the ongoing relationship may be damaged. If there is a further point that really matters to you, then it is likely to be more productive to explain why it merits your joint attention, as an issue that affects both of you. Otherwise you may come across as opportunistic, taking advantage of the other person's co-operativeness.

An alternative move ...

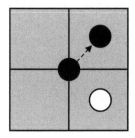

5. Give and take

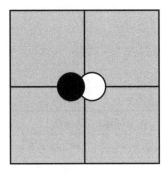

Implicit messages:

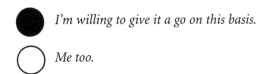 *I'm willing to give it a go on this basis.*

○ *Me too.*

The observer's view: *Flexibility from both parties in the interests of finding a way forward.*

Potential for influential relating: HIGH

Advice: A constructive pattern of interaction, especially when otherwise facing an impasse. However, the risk here is in compromising prematurely without first having thoroughly explored and understood the issues at stake for both parties. Without a grounding of shared understanding of each other's concerns, this mutual give-and-take may leave important matters unresolved and produce a merely temporary solution. The effect can be to compromise the ongoing relationship as well as the immediate issue.

An alternative move …

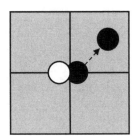

Extracting some principles

Look at the respective impact of the different patterns of interaction in terms of influential relating.

YOU \ Other	Competitive	Avoiding	Accommodating	Collaborative	Compromising
Competitive	LOW	LOW	LOW	LOW	LOW
Avoiding	LOW	MODERATE	LOW	LOW	LOW
Accommodating	MODERATE	HIGH	MODERATE	MODERATE	LOW
Collaborative	HIGH	HIGH	MODERATE	HIGH	HIGH
Compromising	MODERATE	HIGH	LOW	MODERATE	HIGH

The messages are reasonably clear. *Collaborating* is a preferred strategy for influential relating, and both *compromising* and *accommodating* have something to offer. The more dangerous strategies, in terms of influential relating, are competitive and avoiding strategies. This is not surprising since these are essentially less co-operative approaches.

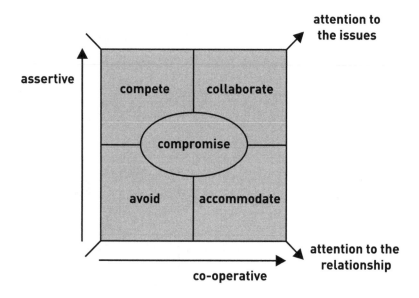

However, no strategy is entirely without risk, because the impact of your approach is always dependent on the posture adopted by the other person. That is why it is important to think in terms of the interaction, the pattern of relating rather than merely in terms of your own approach. It is also why it is vital to recognize when a pattern is proving less productive than an alternative might be. And why it is important to have the repertoire and flexibility to make smart moves to change the pattern of the interaction.

People can have too limited a repertoire, becoming overcommitted to particular approaches, either because they are temperamentally more drawn to some than others, or through sheer force of unexamined habit, or through thinking about their relating too one-sidedly. Many patterns of *interaction* are possible. Some are influential. Others are unproductive or even destructive. Flexibility is therefore essential. So here are some rules of thumb ...

Developing your influential relating

- Self-centred strategies become self-limiting.

- Accommodating and befriending strategies are useful, but potentially fragile, because roles, responsibilities and situations vary, creating occasions when particular issues will be a more pressing consideration than the relationship.

- Collaborative strategies are a good default setting for producing influential relating. Aim to shape your patterns of interaction in this manner, making excursions from it if necessary.

- Approaches need to be congruent, but merely mimicking or mirroring the other person may not yield a productive pattern, and will leave you a follower rather than a leader.

- Take the lead in shaping the pattern of the interaction.

- Pay attention to the impact you are having on others.

- Keep thinking. Stay flexible. Watch what's happening in the interaction; if it isn't proving productive, then be the one who reshapes the pattern.

What else can you do?

Connect the material in this chapter to your own experience, both past and current. That is how to get use and value from it in the future. Here are some questions to help you apply some higher-order thinking to produce higher-order relating.

One approach is to focus on people who are significant for you ...

- Which are key working relationships as far as your career is concerned?
- Focus on one of the most important of these people.
- Think about some of your recent interactions.
- What pattern or patterns did you see in that interaction?
- What happened?
- Might you usefully have reshaped the interaction at some point?
- How?

Alternatively, focus on a particular pattern ...

- When were you most recently in this position?
- With whom?
- What happened?
- What were the consequences?
- How might you have reshaped the interaction?
- When are you next due to meet this person?
- How are you going to shape that interaction?

The key message is this. It is easy to get stuck in a counter-productive pattern. Don't get stuck. If you get stuck in your relating, you'll get stuck in your career.

Where next?

We've looked at the three principal ingredients in the fast track formula. The next task is to look at how they come together in practice. And for you to satisfy yourself that the formula works ...

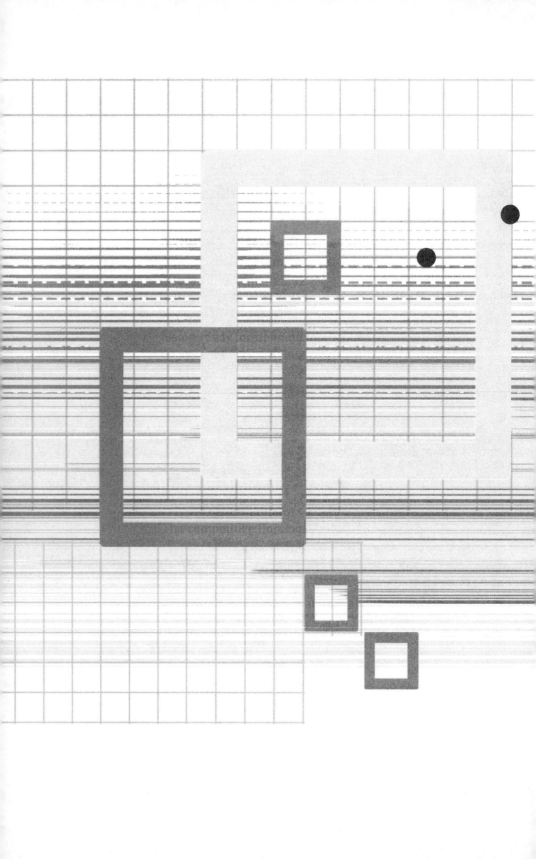

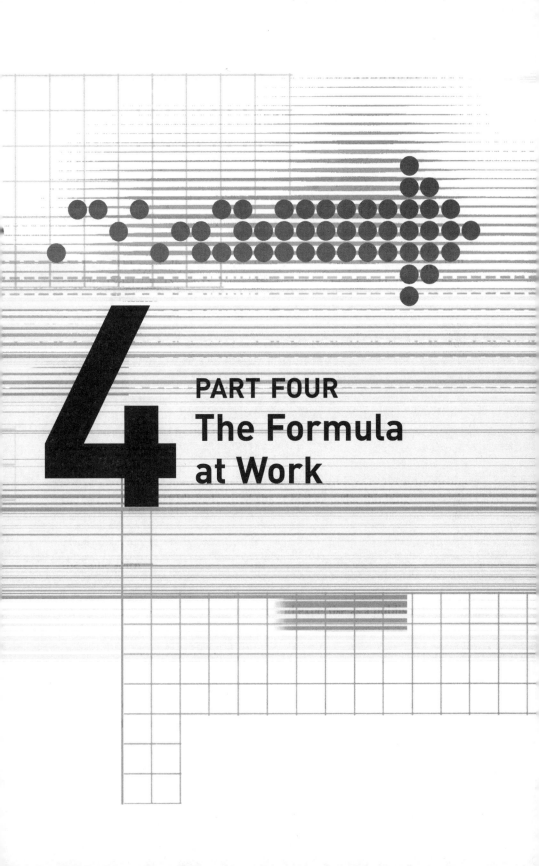

4

PART FOUR
The Formula at Work

6

CHAPTER SIX

Hotspots, Cool Careers

How does career progression really work?

When we embark on our careers, we tend to have an innocent's view about how they will work. We set off with willingness, particularly willingness to learn, in the belief that this will enable us to develop and demonstrate our ability to do the job. The further belief is that this in turn will make us more visible to those who dispense the myriad opportunities that, as we are always assured prior to embarkation, await the enthusiastic and hard-working. The implicit expectation in all this is that ability is duly rewarded with opportunity. All we have to do is to focus on the job in hand, do good work and a virtuous cycle of career progression will be established as our track record and credibility grow and further opportunities follow. It's a naïve view, but energizing while it lasts.

Later in our careers we tend to have acquired a more experienced view. One form of this view is that career progression has nothing whatsoever, or at least nothing much, to do with willingness to learn or even with ability to do the job. Visibility appears to be unrelated to either effort or achievement and the bestowal of opportunities to reflect either favouritism or, worse still, since there is no scope to influence it, sheer random chance. In this scenario it is easy to feel puzzled about your lack of credibility and easier still to feel frustrated, angry or even helpless about your rate of progress. It's an understandable conclusion, but cynical, de-energizing, and consequently largely self-fulfilling.

Another form of the experienced view, and the one on which the fast track formula is based, is, however, more realistic. It works with the same basic building blocks: willingness and ability, visibility and opportunity, credibility and progression. But this perspective traces a more complex set of relationships among these factors. In particular, it recognizes that visibility and opportunity are central, and have a disproportionate effect upon credibility and progression. Hotspots – situations and moments that carry opportunity and visibility, where your ability, willingness and credibility are most severely judged – are pivotal to career progression.

In this perspective opportunity is not simply the outcome of, or the reward for, capability. It is the occasion on which capability is tested. And in this perspective opportunities and visibility are not limited. They are abundant. They don't just take the form of promotions or new jobs, but come at you in many forms, large and small, lengthy and fleeting, projects and assignments, tasks and responsibilities, meetings and conversations, expectations expressed and unspoken, impacts intended and unintentional.

So here is the alternative view of how career progression really works. It is a dynamic that can go in either of two directions. In both cases we come to our careers with enthusiasm to learn and to develop our ability to do the job we've been given, which sooner or later includes working effectively with other people. In the course of going about our work we find ourselves – often suddenly and with little warning – in a variety of hotspots, situations of high visibility. This just happens. When and where may often be accidental. But it is our performance in those episodes, and the way it is judged by others, that is the biggest single determinant of our career progression. If we are judged capable, the career dynamic accelerates upward. If we are judged less than capable, the dynamic falters. Judged less than capable on a few occasions and the spiral collapses, producing a career that is at best doing no more than going round in circles.

There are two implications. First, we'd better know a hotspot when we're in one. Secondly, since we cannot control when hotspots are going to occur, we'd better have developed beforehand the capabilities required for handling them.

Knowing a hotspot when you're in one

We have been visiting hotspots all through this book and the intention throughout has been to make you more alert to them. The difficulty is that your hotspots will be uniquely yours. I can't tell you what or when exactly they will be, but I can give you some idea of where and when they might be. But there's no warranty here. It's an uncertain world. So let's at least improve the odds that you'll recognize them when you find yourself in them.

Here's another map to keep in mind.

There are three big career hotspots and they mirror the fast track formula. More precisely, the fast track formula reflects the set of capabilities required to handle the hotspots. A rapid grasp of context, the peculiarities and subtleties of how it works. Higher-order thinking capabilities, or mental agility, to meet the higher-order thinking challenges that are encountered as work becomes more complex, uncertain and ambiguous. A facility for influential relating, which becomes essential as your own role becomes bigger, involves a greater range of constituents, and leaves you more dependent on others to get work done.

Context, thinking challenges and interaction are all prime sources of hotspots. They are drawn overlapping, because of course they may be linked. For instance, an important interaction may be part of the context of your role and the content of that interaction may present a significant thinking challenge. This overlap can help you to recognize them. So can a more detailed list.

So here's a closer look at hotspots. The lists do not claim to be definitive, and some items could feature on more than one list, but you'll see some themes, and they should make your antennae more sensitive to hotspots.

Contextual hotspots

- A range or change of circumstances.
- A range or change of roles and responsibilities.
- A range or change of organizations or ownership.
- A range or change of directions or policies.
- A range or change of priorities.
- A range or change of bosses or staff.
- A range or change of peers or teams.

Thinking hotspots

- Information or decisions that are complex.
- Information or decisions that involve problem-solving.
- Information or decisions that involve possibilities or opportunities.
- Information or decisions that require interpretation.
- Information or decisions that may be ambiguous.
- Information or decisions that are uncertain or risky.
- Information or decisions that are dynamic and changing.

Interactive hotspots

- Encounters that may involve conflict or disagreement.
- Encounters with anyone more senior than yourself.
- Encounters with groups of people.
- Encounters where people look to you for leadership.
- Encounters where you feel uncomfortable: anxious, uncertain, fearful, embarrassed, distrusting, guilty.

- Encounters where you feel emotional: angry, frustrated, temperamental, disappointed, euphoric, shocked.

- Encounters where you express an opinion.

The bottom line is probably clear. Hotspots can come in many forms. Hot situations. Hot tasks. Hot encounters.

The good news is that you don't need to be able to identify what sort of hotspot it is. You don't need to classify it. This is not a train-spotting competition. There are no prizes for precision of recognition. There are only two things that you need to be able to do.

The first is to recognize it as a hotspot. For others, you are in the glare of the spotlight. Those who will be making judgements about you can see that it's a hotspot. They define them. But you might be, at least for the time being, in blissful ignorance, unwittingly caught in the hotspot, and as much in the dark about it as if you were being viewed through night-vision glasses.

Here are three tips for not being taken unawares.

1 Enter likely hotspots vigilantly.

2 When you feel puzzled or confused, admit it, at least to yourself.

3 When you experience an emotional response, use it as a cue that you're in a hotspot.

The second thing that you need to do, having recognized that you're in a hotspot, is to be able to raise your game. And here's where the news gets better still, because the essence of raising your game is to bring higher-order thinking capabilities to bear on the hotspot.

Let's look at the hotspots map from a slightly different angle. Hotspots are challenges to your capabilities, your ability to grasp context, your ability to meet the mental demands of your work, your ability to relate influentially. But if you look back over the earlier parts of this book, you'll see that the key to handling all these challenges is mental agility, the higher-order thinking dispositions that enable you to figure your way through unfamiliar contexts, tricky work and high-stake interactions alike. Higher-order thinking capabilities are central to the fast track formula.

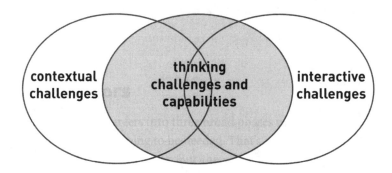

The use and abuse of higher-order thinking

It would be tempting to conclude that the answer is simply to cultivate higher-order thinking, to use it all the time. HOT stuff to cure hotspots! That way, one might reason, you would always be alert to hotspots and be able to handle them effectively. A tempting conclusion, but wrong!

One difficulty is that higher-order thinking requires more effort and takes more time. So it isn't efficient to use it when you don't need to, when you already know your way around a context, for example, or when an interaction is going smoothly and productively. And sometimes you need to act fast. Sometimes near enough is good enough. Sometimes thinking doesn't need to be very organized. That's why the mind tends to default thinking in the first place. But even setting aside the extra effort required, there are many other reasons why the over-use of higher-order thinking can prove counter-productive.

Think about the impact that each of the higher-order thinking dispositions can have when used inappropriately, out of *context*, when the challenge does not require it.

Alert thinking, out of context, will make you come across as over-sensitive, jumpy, neurotic, even paranoid; your views will appear exaggerated, your judgements out of proportion and lacking balance.

A hefty price ticket! But they all are.

Broad thinking, out of context, will make you seem unrealistic, ungrounded, wacky, a fantasist or just plain deluded.

Inquisitive thinking, out of context, will either make it look as if you are intrusive, nosy, speculative, or like someone who wastes time on irrelevancies, or just doesn't get the point.

Deep thinking, out of context, will make you seem fussy, slow, over-complicated, unnecessarily detailed, someone who gets lost in the weeds and can't get the big picture; alternatively, but no better, you'll come across as simply unintelligible.

The best that can be said for critical thinking, out of context, is that it can come over as pessimistic. More commonly it is seen as negative, unhelpful, uncommitted, unwilling to co-operate, unconstructive, condescending, evasive, hostile or even destructive.

You might not think that there could be much downside to a disposition towards clear thinking. However, out of context, carried to excess, an insistence on clear thinking can come across as long-winded, laboured, pedantic, tiresome and even patronizing.

Strategic thinking, out of context, where it does not seem to be necessary or to make sense, can leave the impression that you have some hidden agenda, that you are crafty, manipulative, over-ambitious, even obsessed.

So you don't want to use higher-order thinking out of context! It may raise your visibility, but it won't help your credibility.

It is hotspots that provide the context for higher-order thinking.

And here's a reprise of another point that has been made earlier, but bears repetition. There are hotspots throughout our working lives, at every stage of our careers. But there are more – and hotter – hotspots in higher-level work than in middle-level work, and more in middle-level work than in low-level work. Glance again at the lists of hotspots earlier in this chapter, and relate it to your own career domain, if you are still in any doubt about this. At which level of the career hierarchy are you personally likely to be most exposed to hotspots?

On the other hand, you personally may feel that you're in plenty of hotspots already, whether you've reached the top or not. If so, that is probably a clue that you need to do more work on developing the skills to handle hotspots. So, here's an elaboration of what can go wrong if you don't use higher-order thinking, HOT stuff, in hotspots ...

Without *alert* thinking, in a hotspot, you are likely to overlook something significant, to miss some telling detail. Most disasters occur because a series of people missed a small tell-tale sign. Absence of alert thinking is a failure to raise your mental game when you need to. It is a failure to pay attention to the quality of your thinking, a failure to notice when your thinking has become too hasty, narrow, fuzzy or disorganized to give you a grip on the situation that you are facing.

Without *broad* thinking, in a hotspot, you are likely to proceed much too narrowly, relying on reflex or habit, using tired, clichéd or stale thinking, ignoring other possibilities. Absence of broad thinking is a failure of boldness, a reluctance to go beyond the comfortable or to look for connections.

Without *inquisitive* thinking, in a hotspot, you are likely to make assumptions, to take too much at face value or to accept the readily available but misleading when what is needed is the pursuit of more elusive but revealing connections. Observe how much children gain, surrounded by early life hotspots, through their relentless use of the question, *Why?* Absence of inquisitive thinking is a failure of curiosity, a failure to inquire.

Without *deep* thinking, in a hotspot, your explanations and understandings are likely to be too superficial and consequently unreliable. Your thinking might have been broad and inquisitive, but unless it is deep enough to uncover the subtleties, distinctions and finer points that affect how complex situations actually function, then your sense-making will not prove to have been sound. Absence of deep thinking can reflect a tendency to be indiscriminate, to seize on the first plausible explanation, a failure to think things through systematically.

Without *critical* thinking, in a hotspot, you are likely to accept opinion, hearsay and unsubstantiated assertions, or to make leaps of faith, ignoring inconvenient or contradictory evidence. Your reasoning will be flawed and you personally are likely to come across as illogical, unreasoning, even reckless. An absence of critical thinking is a failure to construct a chain of reasoning, a lack of mental discipline.

Without *clear* thinking, in a hotspot, you are likely to mislead yourself and others. Inaccurate, imprecise, fuzzy, ambiguous, you will not only be personally confused, you will also be misunderstood. Not a great position to be in on either count! The upside, however, is that feeling unclear is one of the strongest, spontaneous internal clues that our mind gives us. If we admit it, it can serve as a free warning signal that we're in a hotspot and need to go to *alert* and start using our other higher-order thinking capabilities to handle it. Absence of clear thinking can reflect limited vocabulary and poor use of language, easy shortcomings to remedy, if you work at them.

Without *strategic* thinking, in a hotspot, you are likely to take too short-term a view, and consequently to be caught unawares, to become a victim or follower of events rather than an initiator or leader of them. You will come across as unprepared, purposeless, uninspired and uninspiring – Aethelred the Unready. Absence of strategic thinking is a failure of anticipation, a failure either to think ahead at all or to do so in sufficient, practical detail. It can reflect a tendency to focus on the present rather than the future. This is an easy habit to acquire in lower-level work with its accent on the here-and-now, and even in middle-level work with its frequent emphasis on resolving competing demands, but a problematic habit for the more forward looking demands of higher-level work.

To put it briefly, higher-order thinking is the vital ingredient in the fast track formula. It is important in its own right, because work demands thought, and higher-level work requires more, and better quality, thought than lower-level work. The capability of higher-order thinking becomes more and more fundamental to success as your career progresses. But it is also vital to the other elements of the formula, the capacity to get to grips with a context and the capacity for influential relating. Without higher-order thinking these capacities would be limited.

Without higher-order thinking, grasp of context would essentially be based on recognition of the familiar. If you had worked in various contexts, and had accumulated know-how within those domains, you would show some range and flexibility to get on top of new situations, but it would be more fragile and limited than the capability that comes with higher-order thinking. Management trainee and other so-called 'fast-track' schemes, which aim to give participants early experience in a wide variety of departments, are designed to address the challenge of changing context that comes with career progression. But without also giving attention to the development of higher-order thinking capabilities, the benefits to be obtained during the course of this breadth of experience will be restricted. The limitations – and costs – of the approach will eventually be exposed, usually when the individual reaches a higher-level position for which past experience alone can never be sufficient preparation.

Without higher-order thinking, the capacity for influential relating also runs out of steam. Relating on the basis of personality, or personal warmth, some sensitivity to others and a willingness to co-operate works reasonably well in the earlier stages of a career. And these characteristics are not unimportant later, when – as we have seen – the nature of the work to be done usually involves a wider range of contacts and relationships, and a greater dependence on others. But consideration for others is not enough. The reason is that the issues involved in higher-level work are more complex. There are more dilemmas, more competing priorities, more uncertainties, fewer if any right answers. There is no easy way through, when satisfying one person means disappointing another, or when the only way forward is into an unknown that everyone – to one degree or another – finds unsettling. Consequently, higher-level work entails influential relating that is based not just on personal relationship but on developing shared understandings of complicated and often difficult issues. For this you need an approach that is simultaneously concerned *and* detached. And relating is dynamic, not stable. It is an ongoing process, particularly in higher-level work with its particular responsibility for shaping the frontier between the present and the future. Higher-order thinking is the key to managing that process.

To give the point more immediacy, and put it more bluntly, if you don't *have and use* higher-order thinking, then your career is likely to fail. Either you'll fail to get on top of a context, or you'll fail to deal with a mental challenge in the mainstream of your day-job, or you'll botch an important piece of relating. You might even do all three! And you may get away with it, on a few occasions, for a while. But remember, visibility has disproportionate impact on career progression. Incompetence makes a stronger impression than ability. Since higher-order thinking is your best protection against appearing incompetent, I recommend learning when and how to use it, and sooner rather than later.

Cool careers

Career tends to be a cool spot in our thinking. While the job we're doing may be at the front of our minds, the career that it is part of tends to sit at the back. Except, occasionally, when we are flicking through the job pages, whether idly, eagerly or anxiously. When we are approached by a 'head hunter', sorry, search consultant. When the repeated frustration of getting stuck in a commuting gridlock finally reaches a tipping point. When something or – perhaps more commonly – someone at work makes us question whether what we are doing is worthwhile. But even then our attention is quickly re-occupied by the current job or by the next possibility rather than by thoughts on the career as such.

This is not surprising. Careers play out over a long time, which makes them hard to keep in mind. Also they include long periods of routine, mundane activity. They are seldom helter-skelter, even the ones which seem as if they must be the most exciting and action-packed. People on active military service frequently describe warfare as long periods of boredom punctuated by short episodes of sheer terror. Percussionist Charlie Watts described his (first) twenty-five years with the Rolling Stones as twenty years hanging around to do five years drumming.

But we want cool careers in the other sense of the word. Careers that will provide us with work that we can enjoy and find properly rewarding, that our friends and others will admire. Careers such that when we get towards the end we can look back on them and feel satisfied that we have made good use of the time – the only time – that we had.

What we don't want is to find ourselves well through our career, still unwrapping the mysterious package, finally, belatedly recognizing all the opportunities that have been missed without us realizing.

The broad point of this book is that it is necessary to go about our careers mindfully. It is both necessary and possible. The more specific points have been about how to do it. We can expect hotspots, we can have a pretty shrewd idea where they might occur, and we can prepare ourselves for the encounters. We can't fully control our careers, because no one can. There will always be elements of chance, and there will always be others who have a hand – or at least a voice – in determining what opportunities we get. But what we can do is improve our prospects of career progression by learning how to be higher-order thinkers and how to use that capability to handle the hotspots in which careers are melted or made. We can do a lot to give ourselves a cool career.

Back to Mr Watts and his colleagues in one of the most successful careers in rock 'n' roll. How do they do it? They haven't had a number 1 single record in decades, but they deliver in the real hotspot. In concert. And even after forty years they still rehearse. A poor example, you might say. A long career doing essentially the same thing rather than a story of career progression. Okay, look at military personnel. How do they prepare for hotspots? How do they prepare to progress through the ranks? Through training. Rehearsal. Like the Rolling Stones in this respect. Career professionals.

And this is the point. Successful careers need attention. Accelerating your career needs your attention. Not in the cool spots, the occasional reflections and musings when you don't have anything else on your mind, but in the hotspots, when your mind is already full. Under pressure. On edge. At the edge.

This whole book has been about how to do that. But here is a final set of tips. A set of higher-order thoughts. To use in the moment. In the hotspots. Some starter thoughts to help you to get to grips with those hotspots. The questions do not claim to be comprehensive. They are aimed to stimulate your own thinking.

For contextual challenges

- How does this differ from where I was before?
- How else can I think about this situation?
- What is curious or interesting about this situation?
- How do things really work around here?
- What am I ignoring or not taking into account?
- How can I explain this situation clearly and concisely to someone else?
- How can I take things forward in this situation?

For mental challenges

- How am I thinking about this task?
- What are a couple of other, different ways of going about this?
- What's puzzling or strange about this?
- How does this fit together and what will happen over time?
- Where are the weak points in my reasoning?

- How can I explain this lucidly in only three sentences?

- What actions can I take and how will the benefits outweigh the costs?

For interactional challenges

- What's happening here?

- How does this interaction look from other points of view?

- What's surprising here?

- What's the reasoning behind that?

- What am I neglecting or discounting?

- How can I express this differently and more clearly?

- What steps can I take from here and where will they lead?

Help comes in the form of questions, when it can't come in the form of answers. Your challenges will be your own. And that is a good point at which to leave you. Thinking about your own hotspots. So, what are they? Can you pinpoint three coming over your horizon? Three hotspots that are real for you, that could either help or hinder your career. Now.

Where next?

You're at a fork in the track. You've got the formula now, so it's a good moment to put the book down and get on with using it. On the other hand, if you'd prefer more convincing that the formula really works in practice, then you might be interested to read about some well-known people in the final chapter.

7

CHAPTER SEVEN

Great Examples

Does the formula work?

Care should always be taken when applying formulas to people. Remember the story of *Dr Jekyll and Mr Hyde*, where the brilliant doctor creates a potion that utterly changes his appearance, personality and behaviour? Or the film *Indiana Jones and the Last Crusade*, where the hero has to save his wounded father by pouring water from the holy grail on to an otherwise fatal gunshot wound? Formulas can be tricky. So, does the fast track formula work?

The easy answer would be to say that you won't know unless you try it. But a higher-order disposition for critical thinking would not be satisfied with that! Besides, you may be concerned that you might turn into Mr Hyde. So the purpose of this chapter is to give you an opportunity to judge the formula for yourself by having a look at some public examples. This should give you some independent evidence.

Corroboration is important. The fast track formula presented in this book grew out of years working in management development and practising as a personal coach. It is the product of observing, discussing, reading around, and making sense of those observations. Unless you've opened the book and started at this point, you'll know the formula by now ...

Rapid grasp of context
plus
Higher-order thinking capabilities
plus
Higher-order interpersonal skills
produces
faster career progression.

But is there any objective support for this proposition? Can we see the formula at work in the careers of people who haven't read this book, but who would generally be accepted as fast-trackers? Let's have a look into some autobiographies of successful people from a variety of different career domains. To let the evidence speak for itself, I've used their words with a minimum of linking commentary of my own to draw out the parallels. See what you think.

The Boy Racer

One person with an obvious claim to being a fast-tracker is Canadian racing driver Jacques Villeneuve. Already a success in IndyCar, this young man burst on to the Formula 1 scene in 1996 with a sensational debut season in which he came second in the championship, losing his bid for the title only in the final race of the year.

The story of that first season is told in his book, *Villeneuve: winning in style* [Collins Willow, 1997]. It yields a series of glimpses of the fast track formula.

We see him setting out to grasp the new context in which he found himself.

One of the main tasks in my first F1 season would be to learn the new circuits ... knowing the track is useful because you don't have to go through the process of discovering where to place the wheels in the corners, where to brake and so on, and you can concentrate on bringing the car up to speed, instead of yourself. (p. 15)

I had to become accustomed to the differences between an Indy car and an F1 car. An F1 car is slower on the straights but much quicker on the corners ... and because an F1 car is lighter and more responsive it reacts to the driver's input. (p. 13)

Every race of my first F1 season was to be a learning experience. (p. 25)

Racing here twice before in Formula 3 was of little use for the realities of Formula 1. It was a totally new experience on what seemed a completely different track that had to be learned as if from scratch. (p. 62)

Did higher-order thinking feature in his adaptation to these new demands?

In the races I learned a lot about tactics and strategy – how to think and plan ahead, to watch what was happening and how to react to it – not just go balls-out on every lap. (p. 30)

The car was twitching on nearly every corner of every lap. It was very treacherous and really easy to get caught out. You had to be extremely alert, and even then there was some luck involved in staying on the road. (p. 71)

You need quick reflexes and fast reaction times and you also have to use your head. Staying on the road requires alertness, anticipation, a certain amount of informed guesswork and also some experimentation. There is no guarantee that conditions will be exactly the same on the next lap, so you have to be flexible in your thinking. It helps if you have a realistic imagination so that you can see in your mind's eye the various options available, and then think fast to choose the right one. (p. 75)

You can't go completely flat out all the time because you have to save a space in your brain to think about the car's reactions. But you have to be going quickly, otherwise you don't get the full picture. (p. 58)

Did his career progression through Formula 3 to F1 require a higher order of interpersonal capabilities?

I learned to work harder, which was a good thing because up until this point I was lazy! The Tom's team didn't speak much English so I had to work harder with the engineers. ... All in all, the extra responsibility changed for the better my way of thinking and working. (p. 30)

To make your feelings known, and to have them translated into setup changes, you need a good relationship with your race engineer and the mechanics. They have to understand how you drive and what you want from the car. When you say to them that the car is performing in a certain way it's not something you will find in a textbook or a dictionary. The communication is something very personal – almost like a private code – that only becomes understood after you've been working together awhile. (p. 109)

The chemistry among the people involved is one of the most important factors in a successful racing team, and ours was getting better and better. The more rapport you have the more productive you become. (p. 46)

The pressures of having to attend to multiple stakeholders come out clearly.

You don't have time for a proper lunch, so you gulp something down quickly, because there are appearances to be made in the sponsors' suites. ... It's always non-stop. (p. 149)

The pressure from photographers and journalists was unbelievable. It started several days before the race and never let up. It was distracting and made it harder to concentrate on racing. But this is the price you pay to be in F1. (p. 27)

To overtake successfully you have to have maximum confidence in your own judgement and also trust the judgement of the other driver. With experience you get to know what to expect from certain drivers. (p. 163)

He had – and recognized the importance of – defining moments.

My start was terrible. The car got off the line well, but only for about a metre and then the engine hit the rev limiter. ... I had somehow failed to release the clutch properly, the power came to the rear wheels about three seconds later than it should have and suddenly I was in ninth position. (p. 36)

Being able to recover quickly from moments of lost adhesion is a big advantage. (p. 74)

Only a few seconds separate you from success or failure. (p. 21)

And the feeling of having – and being on – the edge.

I love the feeling when you're right on the edge and pushing it ... the car gets very light, just short of sliding, and you hold it there. You're really on the limit, you can feel it, and you're controlling it. (p. 55)

You don't have to finish first to feel like a winner. ... Winning is the most important thing, but it's not as big a thrill as pushing the limit and being on the edge. (p. 42)

When you suddenly get sideways you can't tighten up or over-react, nor can you afford to slow down. You always have to keep pushing to the limits of the conditions, while staying within your own capabilities. (p. 74)

Villeneuve's words show a realistic appreciation of the nature and dynamics of career progression.

When you go up the ladder in a series you have to work until it feels as natural as it did in the smaller series. ... The big thing to get accustomed to is the power. ... Everything happens so fast. You're just shifting, braking, turning the wheel – all in a blur. You don't really know what's happening. After about 5 laps you're as tired as you've ever been in a racing car. (p. 32)

The wheel came off because some retaining pins failed to keep a wheel nut in place. There was no point in blaming anyone, it was just a racing incident, the kind of thing that is bound to happen occasionally. (p. 174)

Having a perfect lap is rare. (p. 161)

About as rare as a perfect day in any other career.

Extraordinary – A Popular Politician

The autobiography of Labour politician Mo Mowlam takes us into a very different career domain. Apart from the rare distinction of being an unusually widely respected politician, she is one of what remains a handful of women to achieve a senior position in national government. She became Secretary of State for Northern Ireland in 1997 before the age of forty and she held that office through a period in which significant progress was made, through the Good Friday Agreement and the subsequent Referendum, towards the resolution of its troubles. Moved from that role, because – it has been suggested – her popularity was beginning to rival that of the Prime Minister, she worked in the Cabinet Office and on anti-drugs campaigns, both nationally and internationally, before resigning as an MP in 2001.

Her story is told in her autobiography, *Momentum: the struggle for peace, politics & the people* [Hodder & Stoughton, 2002].

Again we see the importance of getting a good grasp of the specific and complex context of the job. It informs both the thinking and the interpersonal challenges that accompany any career progression.

My first stint in Northern Ireland [as Shadow Minister] gave me a good grounding on the issues for when I returned as Shadow Northern Ireland Secretary in 1994. ... But I learnt most of all from going across every week to talk to people, to listen, and to make contacts. This had the advantage of not only expanding my knowledge, but also of giving me a much better understanding of who, if we were elected, I would be working with. (p. 18)

Debates within Northern Ireland are usually loud and tetchy, conducted at megaphone level. But there is also an insidious background of whispers and mutterings about plots and conspiracies. (p. 117)

I did have a good network of folk from all sides who kept in touch; it gave me, I think, quite a balanced view of what was happening on the ground. (p. 117)

And, likewise, when she came to work with the Colombian Government to tackle international drug-trafficking …

From a starting point of zero information I had to learn fast. I enjoyed the challenge. … After my first visit I had a good sense of how the drugs problems fitted into the overall picture, which was pretty chaotic and very violent. (p. 327)

Mowlam's high-level interpersonal skills have often been credited with keeping the various contending factions at the negotiating table. The importance of relating is certainly evident in her own account of her career.

I often used to get up and serve the tea at these meetings because it helped people to relax and talk. (p. 156)

Many other important relationships were formed in those years in opposition, not least with members of the Irish Government and Irish diplomats and key people in the United States like Senator George Mitchell and the Clintons. I could not have done as much as quickly without all the preparation that went into nearly two and a half years in opposition. (p. 39)

I decided to split my time between the talks and talking to the people outside so that people didn't feel cut out of what was going on in the talks. … It is very important to be as inclusive as possible. (p. 206)

If I am to engage my audience I have to be able to look at them and profoundly interact with them, which is not possible with a written speech. … I know it drove my special advisors crazy. They would write a clear, concise speech and I would gut it, making it wandering and illogical. But it worked, because I engaged with my audience. (p. 248)

Defining moments were essentially interpersonal.

I knew we were making progress when during my meeting with President Khatami [of Iran] we began talking in a more relaxed manner. … At times like that, the number of officials present can be a real handicap to progress, when personal chemistry is so important. (p. 340)

Similarly, in controversially meeting prisoners in the Maze Prison ...

It was really of very little importance what was said – it was the act itself that held meaning for them. (p. 187)

The tricky nature of the unspoken cultural rules that come into play at the highest level are also well illustrated.

I found the constant fight to increase the power and influence of the department dull. It was a game that I was not that interested in playing, much to the disappointment of some of my civil servants. ... But I recognise that not seeing the need for this kind of fight was probably one of my political weaknesses. (p. 325)

Not taking the Department of Health job in the 1999 autumn reshuffle was, I'm sure, another mistake on my part. ... My rejecting what Tony wanted to do with me, for the second time, I'm sure did not help our relationship. (p. 348)

While her interpersonal skills are at the foreground of the story, her appreciation of the importance of meeting the higher-order thinking challenge is also evident.

I and other Shadow Ministers used what spare time there was to think and work out longer-term strategy as well as responding to day-to-day issues as they arose. (p. 18)

It was always frustrating in Government not having enough time to think or write. (p. 361)

Delivery of policy does not come about without proper management and thought about what is needed. (p. 344)

Hillsborough came into its own then. The gardens gave people the space to think and talk in peace. (p. 214)

The least scary [times] were in the middle of the talks when most of my concentration was on making sure my brain was working, as I was so focused on the talks. (p. 69)

In valuing the thinking capabilities of the Talks' chairman, American Senator George Mitchell, she also acknowledges how easy it is to overlook this element of the formula for success.

He carefully thought out moves, sought out what was happening and managed the process much more than anybody ever realised. (p. 151)

Mowlam's autobiography provides wonderful insights into the nature of high-level working, the nature of the territory into which accelerating your career will propel you. Let's just underline it in her own words.

As always, the reality was more complicated. (p. 89)

At times you won't have any guidance or precedents to go on. (p. 311)

The Spy Mistress

Our next subject also devoted her career to public service, but in a very different role. Stella Rimington can reasonably claim to have been a career fast-tracker. Joining MI5, the Security Service, in 1965 as a part-time, two-fingered typist, she reached the top as its Director-General in 1992, the first woman to hold the post. She provides her own account of that career in her book, *Open Secret* [Hutchinson, 2001].

Does her career illustrate the fast track formula?

As you would expect, thinking capabilities were a prominent requirement for career progress in an intelligence agency.

Accuracy, precision and the proper assessment of information are fundamental skills for a security service officer. (p. 95)

Counter-espionage is not a glamorous business. … It is all about painstaking and rigorous analysis, the detailed following-up of snippets of information and perseverance in the face of disappointment. A bit of luck helps of course. But it is not the quick jumping to conclusions and the twisting of the facts to meet the theory. … (p. 117)

She particularly accents the importance of alertness in thinking.

You have to develop the skill of keeping your eye on lots of different things at once. Without having time to focus on anything in much detail, you begin to recognise when something is getting out of place in the big picture … it's what successful senior managers do and hard-pressed working mothers. (p. 114)

Rimington is strikingly able to describe the manner of her own thinking, revealing its applied and practical character.

If I am faced with a problem, I either immediately know what my answer is, or I pick at it, rushing towards it and then retreating, constantly reviewing the information I have, until I've sorted it out to my satisfaction. I do dislike unsolved puzzles and ambiguities of all kinds, including in personal situations. Where others might let things alone, I can't resist trying to sort them out, and that is why I tend often to seek to change the status quo. And I am a very practical person. I don't like to sit around theorising. Above all, I like to get on with things, to get things done. So sorting out muddles and getting facts or information in order is what I really enjoy. (p. 123)

Having a grasp of the context in which these thinking capabilities are being employed, another ingredient in the fast track formula, also appears as an important element in her career story.

What was it that I had and they had seen that made me a success in this rather unusual career? ... It is vital to have balance and common sense and an ability to relate what you are doing to ordinary life. ... (p. 122)

...able and prepared to take personal initiatives and quick decisions, often out on the street, in circumstances where they cannot seek guidance from anyone else and frequently on the basis of inadequate information. (p. 178)

For a time we recruited too many people with intellectual skills, but not enough practical skills ... people who simply lacked the necessary judgement and common sense. (p. 182)

Thinking power. Grounded realism. But what about high-order interpersonal skills, the third element of the fast track formula? It emerged early as an ingredient in Stella Rimington's career progress. As an early appraisal noted,

She is a most acceptable, warm-hearted and engaging colleague ... (p. 110)

She had developed her social skills during her twenties while living in India as part of the British High Commission with her career diplomat husband.

I was quite a different person from the rather anxious, socially unconfident young woman who had set out. I had learned to deal with any social situation. (p. 81)

These skills were to stand her in good stead.

A vital skill of an agent-running officer is to relate to and get on with anyone, whoever they are ... (p. 148)

To do well at agent recruitment you needed a fairly well-developed imagination and good amateur dramatic skills. But none of it was any good unless you could also make a convincing recruitment pitch to your target when the moment came to drop your cover and emerge as an agent of British Intelligence. (p. 153)

Relating was also a hallmark of her leadership as Director-General.

As Director-General my approach was collegiate, a style which I found worked well. ... I encouraged my Directors to behave corporately and not as barons each representing their own fiefdoms. ... We also listened to the advice and experience of people from various walks of life outside the public service; I was determined not to fall into the mistake of earlier days in allowing ourselves to be cut off from the outside world. (p. 252)

There are still too many around who appear to believe that in order to lead, it is necessary to know all the answers to all questions immediately; that listening is a sign of weakness. Such people have little idea how to lead by delegation, how to place power and responsibility at the appropriate level or how to use the skills of the frequently very talented and enthusiastic teams they have assembled around them. (p. 276)

That final point demonstrates Stella Rimington's understanding of how the nature of work changes as a career progresses into the higher levels of work. Her own journey through the levels illustrates this.

Reflecting on her first permanent role as Junior Assistant Officer, *'the bottom rung of this rather humble ladder'* ... (p. 91)

I often wonder why I took the job. ... The truth was that I hadn't seen enough of the dull side of the work to be put off ... (p. 91)

We were not responsible for taking decisions on the information we gathered, which involved making recommendations about whether people should be employed or not. That required sometimes quite difficult judgements about the interpretation and assessment of the information and was regarded as more skilled work, requiring far greater knowledge and experience than we novices had. (p. 95)

In 1983, and only the second woman to do so, she was promoted to Assistant Director, *'the first significant management level in the service'* and …

This period presented some of the most intellectually challenging problems of my career and also proved to be one of the busiest and most interesting … we gave a great deal of thought … to what we should and should not report on. I was fortunate that some of the clearest thinkers in the Service … came to join me in that section, because these were not easy issues … (p. 161)

… later in my career, I became Director of Counter-Terrorism. It sometimes seemed to me then that my job was to sit at my desk and worry, while everyone else was out on the street in difficult and sometimes dangerous circumstances getting on with the work. The truth, of course, is that my job was to make sure that the policies, the planning, the people, the training and the resources were right, and then leave them to get on with the operations, being there and ready to handle the political fall-out whether things went right or wrong. (p. 169)

Like all careers, the pattern was not immediately obvious, but emerged over time.

I didn't look at it as a career and it never occurred to me to see if I could do better elsewhere. (p. 92)

And like all careers, hers had its defining moments, when opportunity and credibility came together, taking her into her first role and her last.

I was walking through the High Commission compound when someone tapped me on the shoulder and said, 'Psst … do you want to be a spy.' What actually happened was that one of the First Secretaries … who I knew did something secret, though I did not know exactly what, as one was not encouraged to enquire about these things, asked me whether, if I had a little spare time on my hands, I might consider helping him out in the office. (p. 67)

… One day, shortly before Christmas, after a meeting, I was asked to stay behind and he [the Director-General] said, 'Congratulations. You are to be the next Director-General.' By then, it did not come as a great surprise to me, but thinking about it now, it is, to say the least, rather strange that no one had thought to ask me if I wanted the job. (p. 241)

The Adventuring Entrepreneur

From a career that took place largely behind the scenes, let's take our final example from one that is very much in the public eye and in a totally different sphere. Richard Branson is probably Britain's best-known and most widely-admired entrepreneur. Leaving school and formal education before he was seventeen, he went on to become a multi-millionaire with business interests that have extended from rock music to airline operation and, through the Virgin brand, much, much more. As if these were not sufficient credentials to make him a fast-tracker, he has also established speed and distance records for high-altitude ballooning and, in power-boat racing, has recovered for Great Britain the coveted Blue Riband for the fastest crossing of the Atlantic Ocean.

So, does Richard Branson's career show the fast track formula in practice?

Clearly, he is a man with a rapid grasp of context. Otherwise he could not have achieved what he has in so many different domains.

It is also clear that he has a great ability to relate. This was evident in the philosophy behind the original Virgin Records shop …

We wanted to relate to the customers, not patronise them. (p. 74)

… and in his business priorities, which put staff first, customers second, and stakeholders third, in the belief that shareholder interests are best served by customer satisfaction, which is best served by standards of service, which is best served by motivated staff.

This is not only a reflection of the importance of our people, it is also the most positive way of fitting together these three priorities. … All my staff have my home address and are encouraged to get in touch. Many do. I make sure that their letters are the very first I answer. (pp. 463–4)

Because he is so clearly a man of action, we are going to concentrate here on the less obvious dimension, on Branson the thinker. His autobiography *Losing My Virginity* [Virgin Books, 1998] provides multiple glimpses of him using higher-order thinking capabilities.

It is quickly apparent that his thinking is **alert**.

I was obviously missing something but I couldn't see what it was. (p. 342)

Ultimately you never know what to expect when dealing with other people ... situations can change. (p. 439)

My most essential possession is a standard-sized school notebook ... ideas are the lifeblood. It is unforgiveable in the course of a meeting or conversation to let them float away uncaptured, to be lost for all time, when with a little effort and so simple a device one can preserve them and bring them back to mind later. (p. 467)

I prefer ... to keep my wits about me. (p. 82)

His thinking is also **broad**, open-minded and creative.

A business has to be involving; it has to be fun, and it has to exercise your creative instincts. (p. 53)

At the other end of the spectrum from buying records – the recording studios – I heard that conditions were extremely formal. Bands had to check in at an appointed time. ... The idea of the Rolling Stones having to record 'Brown Sugar' immediately after breakfast struck me as ridiculous. ... So during 1971 I started looking for a country house that I could convert into a studio. (p. 77)

I have no idea whether Virgin Cola will become a global leader in soft drinks or not. As with all our businesses, I keep an open mind. (p. 437)

I have always enjoyed breaking the rules, whether they were school rules or accepted conventions ... (p. 90)

However, unlike many creative types, Branson also pays attention to the **critical** thinking.

The idea of operating a Virgin airline grabbed my imagination, but I had to work out in my own mind what the potential risks were. ... I wrote out a list of things I wanted to understand about how the aircraft leasing would work. (p. 193)

It is no secret that I love playing devil's advocate. (p. 438)

Once I was convinced that we had protected the downside – which is always my first concern – the other significant question to resolve was whether the move into Virgin Cola really enhanced the Virgin brand name. (p. 438)

The thinking is also **deep** enough to produce a sound understanding of complex situations.

Many outsiders bracket films and music together as 'entertainment', but we quickly learnt that there is a vast difference. ... When we sign a contract with a rock star, the headline figure may appear huge ... but our financial commitment is rolled out slowly. ... With films, our £5 million would be just that: a straight one-off payment which was spent virtually all at once. (p. 191)

... We, the practitioners of the market economy, cannot expect ministers and civil servants to have an intuitive understanding of how markets operate, so we must help them with this understanding. (pp. 468–9)

Being an **inquisitive** thinker clearly helps.

By nature I am curious about life, and this extends to my business. That curiosity has led me down many unexpected paths and introduced me to many extraordinary people. Virgin is a collection of such people and its success rests on them. (p. 435)

I am continually trying to broaden the Group so we are not dependent on a narrow source of income, but I suspect this is more down to inquisitiveness and restlessness than sound financial sense. (p. 180)

Branson's thinking is more than passing curiosity; it is essentially **strategic**, concerned with making plans and pursuing possibilities in practice.

Virgin has always had a life of its own and I have always tried to think ahead with it. (p. 435)

I have always lived my life by making lists: lists of people to call, lists of ideas, lists of companies to set up, lists of people who can make things happen. (p. 441)

My interest in life comes from setting myself huge, apparently unachievable, challenges and trying to rise above them. (p. 195)

His valuing of **clear** thinking is most easily illustrated by how he invokes it when it is most important, in the defining moments, but it is evident that it is also part of Branson's preferred way of thinking.

I had taken so many telephone calls from journalists demanding to know whether our cheques were bouncing that I could barely think straight. I needed some fresh air and privacy so I walked round the lake several times to try to work out what to do. (p. 349)

Whatever I did in the next ten minutes would lead to my death or survival. ... I cleared my mind and concentrated on the options in front of me. I hadn't slept for over 24 hours and my mind felt fuzzy. ... I slapped myself hard across the face to concentrate. (p. 246)

I make notes of all telephone conversations, all meetings, and I draft out letters ... the discipline of writing everything down ensures that I have to listen to people carefully. (pp. 441–2)

Richard Branson would be among the first to challenge the idea of a recipe for success.

There aren't ingredients and techniques that will guarantee success. ... It's not that simple. ... Business is a fluid, changing substance ... (p. 432)

Exactly. That is why developing appreciation of context, attending to relating and investing in higher-order thinking – the elements of the fast track formula – are so vital to progressing any career. As his own career demonstrates.

Where next?

If this book were longer, we would unpack some further examples. But hopefully these four have been sufficient to make the point.

There is good reason to believe that the fast track formula works.

Where you go from here is from other people's careers back into your own and to making the fast track formula work for you.

Beyond the Edge of this Book

The escape clause, maybe ...

You don't have to accelerate your career.

This book is about how to do it, not a directive to do so. How far and how fast you go is also a matter of choice. You can step away from the fast track, pull into the pits, content yourself with a supporting role and leave the racing to others, or go and do something else. Many people do, and are often more content, more fulfilled, and – in their chosen terms – more successful in the process.

To quote one self-employed designer who contributed to my research ...

The focus for the career person is different to that of the mercenary, which in a sense is what I am. The former is concerned with job satisfaction, promotion, responsibility, progress, status, power, ego and the rest of it, while the mercenary concerns himself with money. It is a curiously liberating experience and frees one from the obligations of service, homage, loyalty, gratitude and subsumation that one is obliged to cultivate within a corporate culture.

But a word of warning.

The nature of work is changing. There is reason to believe that the demands of higher-order roles are not simply waiting for you to reach those roles, but are actually coming at you, whether you choose to accelerate towards them or not. Here's the reasoning ...

The traditional assumption was that the distribution of complex work is pyramid-like, with relatively few complex, higher-order roles at the top, and most jobs comprising low-level work at the base. This has changed. Statistical evidence suggests that 'knowledge' work – work involving the mind rather than the hands – now accounts for the bulk of the work done in developed economies, some 60% and rising.

Career patterns are changing. It is already some years since Harvard Business School Professor and organizational theorist, Rosabeth Moss Kanter, pointed the trend out in her book *When Giants Learn to Dance* [Unwin, 1990]. The traditional corporate career revolving around rank and position has been supplemented by other forms, with different dynamics. Progress in the 'corpocratic' career is governed by the accumulation of 'organizational capital': knowing your way around that organization, knowing the right people, knowing the rules of the game. Widespread restructuring and the contracting out of work, however, have led to the emergence of higher proportions of 'professional' and 'entrepreneurial' careers. Professional careers revolve around individual reputation and progress depends on transferable skills. Entrepreneurial careers revolve around the growth, or increase in value, of the entrepreneur's 'territory' and their dynamic is innovation.

More knowledge work. A higher premium on transferable skills. Greater concern for innovation. These shifting contours in the world of work have one shared implication. They place an increasing value on capabilities previously associated with higher- rather than lower-level roles.

You may not want or choose to get to the top, but you may need the capabilities anyway.

Selected Further Reading

The purpose of this book is to alert, enable and encourage you to put the fast track formula into action rather than merely to read about it. This reading list is very selective, with an emphasis on the practical, for any who may wish to pursue particular aspects in greater detail.

Part One: The Nature of the Track

For further insights into the context in which careers are set *The Employment Relationship* by Peter Herriot [Routledge, 2001] is an interesting exploration of some of the different metaphors, both brighter and darker, that people use to express how they feel about the world of employment.

More detail on the levels of work concept can be obtained from *Executive Leadership: a practical guide to managing complexity* by Elliott Jaques and Stephen Clement [Blackwell, 1991].

Part Two: Mental Agility

For much more on thinking dispositions and the improvement of mental performance *Outsmarting IQ: the emerging science of learnable intelligence* by David Perkins [Free Press, 1995] is a masterly exposition of the research by one of the foremost original contributors to the subject.

Edward de Bono has long made the point that the quality of human thinking is constrained by the brain's natural tendency to make quick evaluations with little prior exploration. He has written many books relevant to the development of mental agility, *Six Thinking Hats* [1986], being perhaps the best known. My personal favourites include *PO: beyond yes and no* [1972] and *Simplicity* [1998]. All these titles are published by Penguin Books.

How to Think: building your mental muscle by Stephen Reid [Prentice Hall, 2002] is an accessible introduction to many techniques for deliberately improving the quality of thinking.

The Reflective Practitioner: how professionals think in action by Donald Schön [Basic Books, 1983] is a classic, and the insights provided by the case studies in the second part of the book are fascinating examples of higher-order thinking in practice.

The Logic of Failure: recognising and avoiding error in complex situations by Dietrich Dorner [Perseus, 1996] not only highlights the consequences of failing to meet higher-order thinking demands, but illustrates the warning signs and gives practical steps to rise to the challenge.

Decision Traps by J. Edward Russo and Paul J.H. Schoemaker [Fireside, 1990] is another very readable and pragmatic guide to some of the most common barriers to effective decision-making and how to overcome them.

Learned Optimism by Martin Seligman [Pocket Books, 1998] concerns one of the most important thinking challenges of all, one which can certainly affect careers, how one thinks about oneself. It greatly clarifies the problem of self-limiting thinking.

Part Three: Interaction

Linking personal capability with interpersonal competence is interestingly addressed through the concept of resonance in *The New Leaders* by Emotional Intelligence guru Daniel Goleman, co-writing with Richard Boyatzis and Annie McKee [Little Brown, 2002].

The connections between higher-order thinking and higher-order relating are deeply, practically and entertainingly examined in *King Arthur's Round Table: how collaborative conversations create smart organizations* by David Perkins [John Wiley, 2003].

The *Conflict–Mode Instrument* by Kenneth W. Thomas and Ralph H. Kilmann [Consulting Psychologists Press, 1974] is a self-assessment questionnaire which provides insights into preferred approaches to handling actual and potential disagreements. —

Part Four: The Formula at Work

There are many published autobiographies which illustrate aspects of the fast track formula. The four I chose to use here were:

Branson, Richard (1998) *Losing My Virginity: the autobiography*, Virgin Publishing Ltd

Mowlam, Mo (2002) *Momentum: the struggle for peace, politics & the people*, Hodder & Stoughton

Rimington, Stella (2001) *Open Secret: the autobiography of the former Director-General of MI5*, Hutchinson

Villeneuve, Jacques, with Donaldson, Gerald (1997) *Villeneuve: winning in style*, Collins Willow

Alan Robertson

Supporting transition into higher-level roles

Changing your role, whether or not that involves changing your employer, is one of the most intense and demanding episodes in any career. It is also an increasingly frequent experience in contemporary organizational life. Higher-level work presents multiple challenges, situational, intellectual and interpersonal. Coming into a new role makes these mental and personal demands particularly strenuous. This is why rigorously based executive coaching to facilitate the transition into higher-level work can be so valuable.

Alan Robertson Associates, working in conjunction with selected strategic partners, specialize in the provision of Role Transition Management, a concentrated form of personal coaching, which shortens the adjustment period and accelerates the achievement of performance expectations.

Alan Robertson is an independent management consultant who has advised businesses in a wide range of sectors, including professional services, manufacturing, public utilities, financial services, publishing, education and healthcare. His work is aimed at helping individuals and organizations to meet new and emerging challenges and much of his time is devoted to personal coaching and group facilitation. Alan is an Oxford graduate and an alumnus of the Manchester Business School with further degrees in business administration and psychology. He is a Chartered Fellow of the Chartered Institute of Personnel & Development, a member of the British Psychological Society and a Visiting Lecturer at Cranfield University.

Alan Robertson can be contacted through *changingminds@aol.com*

Also from Prentice Hall Business

FAST THINKING MANAGER'S MANUAL

2nd edition

Manage at the Speed of Life
Ros Jay
£20.00 0273 681052

Back to back meetings, no time to prepare your
report...appraisal...presentation...interview?
What you need is a last minute lifesaver. Fast knowledge is
power and the *Fast Thinking Manager's Manual* is the
ultimate quick reference manual for busy managers who
have a job to do and not enough time to do it.

SIMPLY BRILLIANT 2nd edition

The bestselling guide to getting things done
Fergus O'Connell
£12.99 0273 694456

Simply Brilliant guides you through seven principles to make
even the bright better. Principles of common sense that can
be adapted to attack many of the problems you encounter
every day, in work or outside. With a whole new section on
getting things done in the shortest amount of time.

Sometimes the smart need the simple to be truly brilliant.

**Available at all good bookshops and online at
www.pearson-books.com**

TOM PETERS – LIVE IN LONDON

Tom Peters
£14.99
CD 0273 693972 Cassette 0273 693034

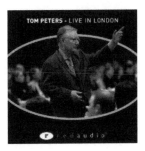

In these disruptive times, leadership is the hottest
management topic. Listen to the world's leading
management guru in one of his most powerful and
inspiring seminars on leadership.

**A full range of Red Audio titles is available
from www.pearson books.com/audio**

Also from Prentice Hall Business

THE RULES OF WORK

A definitive code for personal success
Richard Templar
£9.99 0273 662716

This is the definitive code for personal success, while remaining a decent person. For the first time, this book reveals the hidden competitive advantage of 10 immutable laws followed by high achievers worldwide. Give yourself the edge at work – learn to play by The Rules. Get it, and get ahead.

HOW TO BE A COMPLETE AND UTTER FAILURE IN LIFE, WORK AND EVERYTHING

39½ steps to lasting underachievement
Steve McDermott
£9.99 0273 661663

This is the ultimate "un-improvement" guide, offering 39½ steps to being a failure. Using the power of reverse psychology McDermott shows you how to be an unqualified success.

HOW TO MANAGE YOUR BOSS

Developing the perfect working relationship
Ros Jay
£12.99 0273 659316

Bosses are human – some good, some bad. They have a huge impact on your job satisfaction, your day-to-day happiness, your workload – and yes – your income. If you're lucky they will be understanding, supportive, encouraging and inspiring. Then again they might be lazy, unmotivated, weak, over-emotional, sarcastic, rude, or just downright – well – bossy. We've all got one. It's time to learn how to manage them back.

If you wish to find out more about any of these titles or view our full list visit us at: www.pearson-books.com

PERSONAL NOTES